Write Your Novel Step by Step

By Melanie Anne Phillips

Published by Storymind Press

Copyright 2013 Melanie Anne Philips

All Rights Reserved

Write Your Novel Step by Step

By Melanie Anne Phillips
Creator StoryWeaver Co-creator Dramatica

Introduction

If you are looking for a method to get your novel written, this book will take you step by step from concept to completion. Simply follow the instructions and by the time you are finished, you will have written your book.

At the end of the process, you'll have a fully developed story filled with memorable characters, a riveting plot, powerful theme, and a new spin on your genre.

Each step asks you to consider or perform just one task that moves your novel a step closer toward being a finished book. In this way, no step is ever confusing or too complex and yet your story is ever growing and evolving as you go.

Some steps are informational, and others direct you to write, re-write, or work out a concept for your story. The first step is an informational one and outlines the overall method, which is divided into four key stages in the story development process.

So without further introduction, turn the page to begin step 1.

Inspiration

Part One:
Plot

~ Step 1 ~

Stages of Writing a Novel

Writers often begin the novel development process by thinking about what their story needs: a main character/protagonist/hero, a solid theme, a riveting plot and, of course, to meet all the touch points of their genre.

Because this is just the beginning of the process, they usually don't have much of that worked out yet. And so, they are faced with the daunting task of figuring out their story's world, who's in it, what happens to them, and what it all means before they even write a word. This can throw a writer into creative gridlock right out of the gate and can get so frustrating that the Muse completely desserts them.

Fortunately, there's a better way. Rather than asking what the story needs, we can turn it around and ask what the author needs. What is the most comfortable sequence of activities that will lead a writer from concept to completion of their novel or screenplay?

As varied a lot as we writers are, there are certain fundamental phases we all go through when coming to our stories. In fact, we can arrange the entire creative process into four distinct stages:

1. Inspiration

2. Development

3. Exposition

4. Storytelling

The Inspiration Stage begins the moment we have an idea for a story. This might be an overall concept (*computer geeks are transported to the old west*), a plot twist (*a detective discovers he is investigating his own murder*), a character situation (Ponce de Leon still lives today), a thematic topic (fracking), a character study (an aging rock star who is losing his licks) a line of dialog (*"Just cuz somthin's free don't mean you didn't buy it."*), a title (*Too Old To Die Young*) or any other creative notion that makes you think, *that's a good idea for a story!*

What gets the hair on your writerly tail to stand up isn't important. Whatever it is, you are in the Inspiration Stage and it lasts as long as the ideas flow like spring runoff. You might add characters, specific events in your plot or even write a chapter or two. A very lucky writer never gets out of this stage and just keeps on going until the novel is completely written and sent out for publication.

Alas, for most of us, the Muse vanishes somewhere along the line, and we find ourselves staring at the all-too-familiar blank page wondering where to go from here. Where we go is to Stage Two: Development.

In the Development Stage we stand back and take a long critical look at our story. There are likely sections that are ready to write, or perhaps you've already written some. Then there are the holes, both small and gaping, where there's a disconnect from one moment you've worked out to the next one, bridging over what you can intuitively feel are several skipped beats along the way. There are also breaks in logic when what happens at the beginning makes no sense in connection to what happens at the end (like the Golden Spike if the tracks were a mile apart). There are characters that don't ring true, unresolved conflicts, and expressed emotions that seem to come out of nowhere. You may find thematic inconsistency or may even be missing a theme altogether.

And so, the work begins – tackling each and every one of these by itself, even while trying to make them all fit together. By the end of the development stage, you'll have added detail and richness to your story and gotten all the parts to work in concert like a well-turned machine, but it probably wasn't easy or pleasant.

Eventually (thank providence) you'll have all the leaks plugged and a fresh coat of paint on the thing. You now know your story inside and out. But, your readers won't. In fact, you realize that while you can see your beginning, ending and all that happens in between in a single glance, all at once, your readers or audience will be introduced to the elements of your story in a winding sequential progression of reveals. You also realize you have quite unawares stumbled into Stage Three: Exposition.

You know your story, but how do you unfold it for others? Where do you begin? Do you use flash backs or perhaps flash forwards? Do you mislead them? Do you keep a mystery? Do you spell things out all at once, or do you drop clues along the way?

There are endless techniques for revealing the totality of your story, many can be used simultaneously, and each one adds a different spice to the journey. Like a parade, every float and band has a position designed to create the greatest impact. And when you have all that figured out, you are ready to write as you begin the Storytelling Stage.

Storytelling is all about word play and style. Whether you are writing a novel, a screenplay or a stage play, there are media-specific manners of expression and conventions of communication, but within those there is plenty of room to maneuver artistically.

Before we send it out the door, we writers shift and substitute and polish until (almost regretfully) we let it go, just like a parent bundling up a child for school. In the end, as Da Vinci's famous saying goes, "Art is never finished, only abandoned."

So, Inspiration, Development, Exposition and Storytelling are the four stages of story development that nearly every writer travels through on the way from concept to completion.

In Step 2 we'll explore *Stage One: Inspiration* to discover tips, tricks and techniques for coming up with ideas for your characters, plot, theme and genre.

~ Step 2 ~

Get Out of My Head!

In this step, we'll begin with the first stage, *Inspiration*, and learn how to clear the decks and set a good foundation for all your work to come.

When beginning a new novel, writers are often faced with one of two initial problems that hinders them right from the get go. One – sometimes you have a story concept but can't think of what to do with it. In other words, you know what you want to write about, but the characters and plot elude you. Two – sometimes your head is swimming with so many ideas that you haven't got a clue how to pull them all together into a single unified story.

Fortunately, the solution to both is the same. In each case, you need to clear your mind of what you *do* know about your story to make room for what you'd *like* to know.

If your problem is a story concept but no content, writing it down will help focus your thinking. In fact, once your idea for a novel is out of your head and on paper or screen, you begin to see it objectively, not just subjectively.

Often just having an external look at your idea will spur other ideas that were not apparent when you were simply mulling it over. And at the very least, it will clarify what it is you desire to create.

If, on the other hand, your problem is that all the little thoughts, notions or concepts that sparked the idea there might be a book in there somewhere are swirling around in a chaotic maelstrom.... well, then writing them all down will make room in your mind to start organizing that material by topic, category, sequence, or structural element.

For those whose cognitive cup runneth over, the issue is that one is afraid to forget any of these wonderful ideas, or to lose track of any of the tenuous or gossamer connections among them. And so, we keeping stirring them around and around in our minds, refreshing our memory of them, but leaving us running in circles chasing our creative tales.

By writing down everything your are thinking, not as a story per se, but just in the same fragmented glimpses in which they are presenting themselves to you, you'll be able to let them go, one by one, until your mental processor has retreated from the edge of memory overload and you can begin to pull your material together into the beginnings of a true proto-story.

Whether you are plagued by issue one or two, don't try to fashion a full-fledged story at this stage while you are jotting down your notions. That would simply add an unnecessary burden to your efforts that would hobble your forward progress and likely leave you frustrated by the daunting process of trying to see your finished story before you've even developed it.

Sure, before you write you're going to need that overview of where you are heading to guide you to "The End". But that comes later. For now, in this step, just write down your central concept and/or all the transient inspirations you are juggling in your head.

In step 3, we'll look at what to do with what you've written down...

~ Step 3 ~

What's the Big Idea?

In **Step 2**, we explored the purpose of and methods for clearing your mind by jotting down any initial ideas you may have before trying to further develop your novel. In this step, your goal is to be able to write a single sentence that expresses the essence of what your story is about.

Having a core concept will provide you with a creative beacon – a lighthouse by which to navigate your creative efforts so they stay on course to your ultimate purpose: a completed novel.

While this seems fairly simple, it can be a lot harder than it looks. It is the rare writer who has a focused concise story concept right from the beginning. Many discover the essence of their novel during the development process or even as they write.

As described in step 2, most writers fall into two categories: those with a general sense of what they want to write about and those with a collection of story elements they'd like to include. Some writers have both, but still no solid center to it all.

Without a core concept, the first inclination is to try to pull all the good ideas they have for their novel into a single all-encompassing story. Problem is, people think in topics more easily than they think in narratives. And while all the material may belong to the same subject matter category, more often than not it doesn't really belong in the same story.

Still, no one likes to abandon a good idea – after all, they aren't that easy to come by. And so, writers stop coming up with new ideas as their attention turns more and more toward figuring out how to connect everything they already have.

This can create an every growing spiral of structural complexity in the attempt to fit every notion and concept into a single unifying whole. And before you know it, your inspiration and enthusiasm have both run dry to be replaced by creative frustration with a candy coating of intellectual effort that is not unlike trying to build a single meaningful picture from the pieces of several different puzzles.

To determine the central vision for your novel try these techniques. First, shift your focus from what your story needs, and ask yourself what you need. More precisely, consider why you want to write this story in the first place. What is it that excites you most about this subject matter? Is it a character, a plot line, a thematic message or topic, or just a genre or setting or timeframe or…?

Refer to the list you created in step 2 of your general concept and/or all the elements you have been pondering to possibly include in your story. Next, consider your own *personal* interests and prioritize that list, putting the items you most want to include at the top and those less compelling at the bottom.

(Tip: sometimes it is hard to pick the most interesting and it is

easier to start at the bottom of the list with the least interesting and work up!)

Now, block the bottom half of the list to see only the top items. These are the aspects of your story that are most inspiring to you and represent the heart of your story. Think about them as a group and see if you can perceive a common thread.

This common thread is called a *log line*. Log lines are like the short descriptions of a program you see in cable or satellite television listings. As examples, here are the log lines for two stories of my own:

Snow Sharks (Don't Eat Red Snow) - A group of rich teenage ski-bums are terrorized by escaped sharks that have been genetically altered by the U.S. government to act as mobile land mines in potential arctic wars.

House of W.A.C.S. – In 1942, this cross between Animal House and The Dirty Dozen follows one of the first groups of young women in the newly created Women's Army Corps as they learn to work together as a team to thwart a Nazi fifth column and protect a crucial war factory.

Using these as a guide, try to write a sentence that describes the core concept you see in your work from step 2.

If your material is too limited or sketchy, just describe the idea that has you excited enough want to write this particular novel, such as:

I'm fascinated with the notion of an archeologist finding a modern device embedded in the ruins of an ancient civilization.

If you have the opposite problem and your wealth of story ideas is so wide-ranging or diffuse to easily see the thread, try writing several log lines, each of which touches on one aspect of what you see in your step 2 work.

Each of these sub-log lines will help focus a different part of what you'd like your story to be. So, rather than trying to find the core directly from your original list, try to see the central concept outlined by your collection of log lines.

Hopefully, by using some or all of these techniques, you'll be able to answer the question, *What's the Big Idea?* But if you can't, don't worry. Some writers need to add to their collection of story elements before the big picture emerges.

In step 4, we'll walk through a really useful method for using your existing concepts as seeds from which to grow new ideas. So, if you don't yet have a log line, you soon will as you begin to integrate this additional material into your evolving story.

~ Step 4 ~

The Creativity Two-Step

In Step 3, we described methods for boiling your initial story concepts down into a *log line*: a single sentence that expresses the essence of what your story is about.

In this step, we'll use your log line as a creative core in a method that will generate an expanding sphere of new ideas for your story. In following this step, also draw upon the original story ideas you jotted down in **Step 2**.

The concept behind this method of finding inspiration is quite simple, really: It is easier to come up with many ideas than it is to come up with one idea.

Now that may sound counter-intuitive, but consider this... When you are working on a particular story and you run into a specific structural problem, you are looking for a creative inspiration in a very narrow area. But creativity isn't something you can control like a power tool or channel onto a task. Rather, it is random, and applies itself to whatever it wants.

Creative inspiration is always running at full tilt within us, coming up with new ideas, thinking new thoughts – just not the thoughts we are looking for. So if we sit and wait for the Muse to shine its light on the exact structural problem we're stuck on, it might be days before lightning strikes that very spot.

Fortunately, we can trick Creativity into working on our problem by making it think it is being random. As an example, consider this log line for a story: A Marshall in an Old West border town struggles with a cutthroat gang that is <u>bleeding the town dry.</u>

Step One: Asking Questions

Now if you had the assignment to sit down and turn this into a full-blown, interesting, one-of-a-kind story, you might be a bit stuck for what to do next. So, try this. First ask some questions:

1. How old is the Marshall?

2. How much experience does he have?

3. Is he a good shot?

4. How many men has he killed (if any)

5. How many people are in the gang?

6. Does it have a single leader?

7. Is the gang tight-knit?

8. What are they taking from the town?

9. How long have they been doing this?

You could probably go on and on and easily come up with a hundred questions based on that single log line. It might not seem at first that this will help you expand your story, but look at what's really happened. You have tricked your Muse into coming up with a detailed list of what needs to be developed! And it didn't even hurt. In fact, it was actually fun.

Step Two: Answering Questions

But that's just the first step. Next, take each of these questions and come up with as many different answers as you can think of. Let your Muse run wild through your mind. You'll probably find you get some ordinary answers and some really outlandish ones, but you'll absolutely get a load of them!

a) How old is the Marshall?

a. 28

b. 56

c. 86

d. 17

e. 07

f. 35

Some of these potential ages are ridiculous – or are they? Every ordinary story based on such a log line would have the Marshall be some common age from our example list, such as 28 or 35: just another dull story, grinding through the mill.

Step One Revisited

But what if your Marshall was 86 or 7 years old? Let's switch back to Step One and ask some questions about his age.

For example:

c. 86

1. How would an 86 year old become a Marshall?

2. Can he still see okay?

3. What physical maladies plague him?

4. Is he married?

5. What kind of gun does he use?

6. Does he have the respect of the town?

And on and on...

Return to Step Two

As you might expect, now we switch back to Step Two again and answer each question as many different ways as we can.

Example:

5. What kind of gun does he use?

a) He uses an ancient musket, can barely lift it, but is a crack shot and miraculously hits whatever he aims at.

b) He uses an ancient musket and can't hit the broad side of a barn. But somehow, his oddball shots ricochet off so many things, he gets the job done anyway, just not as he planned.

c) He uses a Mini-Gatling gun attached to his walker.

d) He doesn't use a gun at all. In 63 years with the Texas Rangers, he never needed one and doesn't need one now.

e) He uses a sawed off shotgun, but needs his deputy to pull the trigger for him as he aims.

f) He uses a whip.

g) He uses a knife, but can't throw it past 5 feet anymore.

And on and on again...

Methinks you begin to get the idea. First you ask questions, which trick the Muse into finding fault with your work — an easy thing to do that your Creative Spirit already does on its own — often to your dismay.

Next, you turn the Muse loose to come up with as many answers for each question as you possibly can.

Then, you switch back to question mode and ask as many as you can about each of your answers.

And then you come up with as many answers as possible for those questions.

You can carry this process out for as many generations as you like, but the bulk of story material you develop will grow so quickly, you'll likely not want to go much further than we went in our example.

Imagine, if you just asked 10 questions about the original log line and responded to each of them with 10 potential answers, you'd have 100 story points to consider.

Then, if you went as far as we just did for each one, you'd ask 10 questions of each answer and end up with 1,000 potential story points. And the final step of 10 answers for each of these would yield 10,000 story points!

Now in the real world, you probably won't bother answering each question — just those that intrigue you. And, you won't trouble yourself to ask questions about every answer — just the ones that suggest they have more development to offer and seem to lead in a direction you might like to go with your story.

The key point is that rather than staring at a blank page trying to find that one structural solution that will fill a gap or connect two points, use the Creativity Two-Step to trick your Muse into spewing out the wealth of ideas it naturally wants to provide.

Your goal for this step, then, is to apply the Creativity Two-Step to your original log line and follow your Muse as far as she can take you. More than likely, you'll end up with something of a mess – a disorganized mash-up of a huge number of story ideas of many different kinds for your novel.

In step 5, we'll delve into the treasure trove of ideas you've generated and begin the process of organizing them into Characters, Plot, Theme, and Genre elements to be further expanded before we move into the Development stage.

~ Step 5 ~

Pulling It All Together

In **Step 2**, you jotted down any and all story ideas you may have already had for your novel. In **Step 4**, you probably generated a huge number of additional creative ideas for your novel. (If not, repeat Step 4 until you do!)

Problem is, the resulting collection of notions for your story from Steps 2 and 4 probably ranges far and wide, resulting in a hodgepodge of interesting concepts and schemes, all out of order and jumbled up in something of a chaotic mess.

So, before we go on into future steps, we need to do a little necessary housekeeping lest things get out of hand. Just as we boiled down your **Step 2** ideas into a single log line, in this step we'll pull together all the material you've created so far into a more manageable form: a *synopsis* of your novel,

A synopsis is like a map of the ground your story is going to cover, noting all the landmarks and important things that happen at them. Just as we originally had you jot down any ideas you already had in Step 2 and then boil them down to a single log line in step 3, we're now going to take all the creative concepts you spewed out in Step 4 and pull them together into a this single conversational description of your novel's content.

The length of a synopsis is completely variable. The shortest form would be a thumb-nail sketch, perhaps just a paragraph long – the minimum necessary to outline the key elements and scope of your story. Typically, the longest synopsis is usually no more than a page or two, though can be *far* more extensive than that.

So, don't feel compelled to write more than comfortably flows or to limit yourself to less than you have. Tolkien, for example, created whole worlds, histories, cultures, and languages in synopsis form before putting any of it in story form.

Our goal here is simply to take that unwieldy shopping list of story elements from Steps 2 and 4 and to turn it into conversational language that, more or less, describes all the interesting people, events, topics, and stylistic flourishes you'd like to include in your novel, as if you were talking about your story to a friend, rather than actually trying to tell your story.

So, for this step, your task is to refer to all that you created so far and describe it as if you were telling someone about your story who was very interested in it and wanted to hear every juicy detail.

"My novel is about...." There. I started it for you. Now, go to town. Guided by your log line that describes the crux and center of your novel's concept, write your synopsis of every interesting and/or essential thing that is going to be in it, based on the work you've done in the last step.

Sample Synopsis (from my own work):

Snow Sharks: Don't Eat Red Snow

The government has been developing a new breed of shark that lives in snow rather than water for use as mobile land mines in places such as Siberia or the Arctic. A transport plane carrying them crashes in a storm high in the Rocky Mountains, just above a high-priced ski resort for the rich.

Normally closed at this time, the resort was opened for a powerful client so that his college-age daughter and her friends could have a ski vacation. The sharks gradually slither down from the heights into the bowl-shaped resort and begin feasting on the kids.

Characters include the handsome but stupid jock, the stuck-up daughter of the patron, a cheerleader, a nerdy science geek who is the tag-along token outcast, and the usual crew of stereotypical college kids.

Scenes include night skiing where the proprietors had installed disco lights on the ski run, so they light up and create changing colored patterns under the snow. During the night skiing, we see one of the kids ski by, followed by a silhouette against the disco lights of a snow shark following him. This is the first attack that alerts them that something deadly is out there on the slopes.

In a later scene, the jock trying to escape by out-skiing the others, leaving them to die, when the sharks attack. He ski-jumps over a chasm, looks back and laughs, looks forward and a snow shark has also jumped the chasm by shooting down the hill on the other side and is coming right for him. The skis land solidly on the other side of the chasm with nothing but boots attached, and bloody stumps sticking out of them.

The government sees this as a great opportunity to see how effective the sharks are and send in an agent to document but not interfere. He ends up dying a horrible death that both divulges to the kids what the government has done and provides the idea of how to escape.

Ultimately, they learn the sharks can no longer live in water, only in snow, so they blow up a geothermal spring to flash-melt the snow above the bowl-shaped valley, ironically drowning the sharks, and barely escaping the floodwaters themselves.

Armed with this rather cliché example, it's time to write the first synopsis for your own novel. As we continue through our step by step method, we'll pause after each major new creative effort to fold what you've just developed into a revised synopsis. In this way, you have a story right from the beginning that is continually evolving, step by step, into your finished novel.

Next, in Step 6, we'll stand back a bit to see the first draft of your synopsis just as your readers will, looking for any holes they might see. Then in the step after that, we'll begin to fill them.

~ Step 6 ~

Pulling It All Apart

In Step 5, you created your first comprehensive description of what your story is about – who's in it, what happens to them, what it all means, and the *story world* in which it all takes place.

In this step you'll take a new look at this synopsis to find holes in your story – dramatic elements that are either missing or inconsistent with one another.

For a moment, step out of your role as author, and put yourself in the position of your reader or audience. Read over your story synopsis from Step 5. If something doesn't make sense, is off kilter or missing, make a note of it.

List each point in the form of a question, as this tends to help you focus in on exactly what is needed to fix the problem.

When you have finished your novel, your audience will be

unforgiving, so be harsh now! Don't gloss over problems, but don't try to solve them either. That comes later.

For now, just ask questions about everything that bothers you about your story from a reader's perspective, as if you were reading someone else's description of their story rather than your own.

If push comes to shove and you are just too close to your story to see many problems with it, share your synopsis with friends, family or fellow writers.

Don't ask them what they think of it – they'll always pull their punches to be kind. Instead, just tell them to write down any questions they have about your story that weren't answered in the synopsis – anything they didn't quite understand or found confusing.

Having them state these issues as questions will get you a far better result than just asking their opinion, for they would really like to know the answers. Friends and family are especially much more likely to be frank if they are just asking questions rather than criticizing.

Using the example below (based on the *Snow Sharks* example synopsis provided for Step 5) pick your synopsis apart as thoroughly as you can, jotting down every question about it that comes to mind.

Example:

Questions About *Snow Sharks*

From the synopsis:

The government has been developing a new breed of

shark that lives in snow rather than water for use as mobile land mines in places such as Siberia or the Arctic.

Questions:

1. What branch of the government is involved?
2. Is this sanctioned or rogue?
3. Who is/are the scientists behind this?
4. How long has this program been going on?
5. How close are they to a final "product?"
6. Do the sharks breathe air?
7. Do they require cold (can they live in heat)?

From the synopsis:

A transport plane carrying them crashes in a storm high in the Rocky Mountains.

Questions:

1. What kind of plane?
2. How many sharks was it carrying?
3. Do they all survive?
4. Where was the transport taking the sharks?
5. Why couldn't they wait until after the storm?
6. How many crewmembers are on board?
7. What are their jobs?
8. Do the crew members know what they are carrying?
9. Do any sharks survive?
10. If so, do the sharks kill all the survivors?
11. Is there anything in the wreckage that reveals the cargo, its nature and who is behind it?
12. Is the crew able to contact their command center before crashing?
13. Are they able to convey their location?
14. Is there a rescue beacon?

15. Does the plane carry a "black box."

Using this list as a guide, separate your entire Step 5 synopsis into short sections (as above) and then come up with as many questions as you can (within reason) about each section.

Next, in Step 7, we'll take each question, one at a time, and generate several potential answers that would satisfy them, thereby expanding and enriching your evolving story, even while you fill its holes and fix its inconsistencies.

~ Step 7 ~

Filling the Holes

In Step 6, you found holes and inconsistencies in your story as it stands so far by looking at it as an audience would, rather than as an author, and asking questions about what was missing or didn't make sense.

In this step you'll fill those holes and fix the inconsistencies by answering these questions to make your story more complete and to tune it up so it rings true.

Recalling the "Creativity Two-Step" method you employed in Step 4, you can see that the questions you've just asked about your synopsis are the first part of that technique. Just as before, your task in this step is to come up with as many potential answers for each question as you can (within reason).

And speaking of reason, just a reminder that the "two-step" method works because it alternates between logic and passion; between the analytical mind and the creative mind.

Asking questions about your synopsis is an analytical endeavor: you are trying to make sense of the story and noting everything that doesn't.

Coming up with a grab bag of answers for each is a creative endeavor: you are turning your Muse loose to invent new concepts with no restrictions at all.

It is important to keep in mind that any answer is a good one, even if it is patently ridiculous. No matter: the most nonsensical idea, though it may never be used itself, can spur the inspiration of just the idea you need, which never would have occurred to you if you hobble your Muse in advance and force it to work within constraints of any kind.

The Muse hates limits, and cannot be directed any more than one can herd cats. Asking the questions is a focused and critical process, but answering them should always be completely free-form in order to achieve the best results.

So, refer to the questions about your story synopsis you just asked in the last step and see how many interesting answers you can bring forth. The more unusual the answer, the more likely your story will avoid following a cliché path and will stand out as original and intriguing.

Example:

Answers to Questions About *Snow Sharks*

From the synopsis:

> A transport plane carrying them [the snow sharks] crashes in a storm high in the Rocky Mountains, just above a high-priced ski resort for the rich.

Questions:

1. What kind of plane?

   a. Constellation
   b. B-2 Bomber
   c. Modified 747
   d. B-17
   e. Blimp
   f. Dirigible
   g. Bi-Plane
   h. Glider
   i. Rebuilt flying saucer from Area 51

2. How many sharks was it carrying?

   a. 1
   b. 17
   c. 300
   d. A mating pair

3. Do they all survive?

   a. Only one survives
   b. 6 survive
   c. They all survive

    d. Just the mating pair
    e. An even dozen

4. Where was the transport taking the sharks?

    a. Hawaii (for disposal)
    b. An arctic research station
    c. A secret base in Colorado
    d. Russia (they were being stolen)
    e. To NASA for a mapping expedition on one of Jupiter's moons.

You may have noticed that a few of the answers actually provide more information than was asked for in the questions, for example:

> Question 4 - Where was the transport taking the sharks?
>
> Answer d. - Russia (they were being stolen)

When I answered "Russia" arbitrarily, I thought of the Russian Mob, and it occurred to me that organized crime might be trying to hijack and resell these biologic weapons.

If additional material comes to mind when answering a question, don't be afraid to include it just because it goes beyond the expected answer. It's all part of the creative process, and it never pays to squelch a good idea.

The more questions you answer, the fewer holes and inconsistencies in your story, and the more answers you come up with, the less cliché your story is likely to be.

Conversely, don't feel pressured to answer everything and never – absolutely NEVER – do more work that you find interesting and pleasurable. The best way to kill a story is to kill your interest in writing it.

Though producing more answers enriches your novel, it may also deplete your drive to get your novel completed if the process becomes work and ceases to be fun.

So, let your Muse loose, without restrictions *or* quotas, and whatever shakes out will both add to your story and add to your motivation to tell it.

Now - spice up your story by peppering it with new material! Then, in Step 8, we'll put it all together and integrate your original concepts and best new ideas into a revised synopsis.

~ Step 8 ~

Putting It Back Together

If you've been diligent in the last step and generated a lot of answers, you probably have a huge number of potential story points. But which ones to use?

Usually, you won't be able to select two answers for the same question, as they would conflict. What's more, some answers for one question might conflict with several from other questions.

The time has come to make some hard choices. In preparation for this, you need to get a good feel for all the potential directions your story might take depending upon which answers your choose to include.

When you came up with your answers, you were probably focusing on each question, one at a time, not on your story as a whole. So, the first thing is to stand back again, read over all the questions and answers from top to bottom straight through at least once or until you have a really good sense of what this grab back has to offer.

Now answer just one more essential question – how married are you to the original story concept you started with? If you really want to tell that original story, then go through your list of questions and answers and eliminate any that aren't compatible with your initial concept.

Once you've completed this task, you can move on to Step 9.

But, if you are falling in love with some of the new potentials that have opened up, then go through your list and mark all the answers that you'd really like to include. Next, prioritize them as to which ones you are most excited about.

What you now have is a list of your very best and most interesting new creative concepts. Problem is, though they all have the same roots, they have diverged and may no longer be able to fit in the same story.

And this is where the hard choices come in. You need to pick one of all possible combinations of these new story points that is compatible both with your story concept and with each other.

There's no easy way to do this. If you really like one new idea so much that you'd rather have it than any combination of others, then choose it first. Next, add your second most favorite new concept that is not incompatible with the first, and so on, until you have selected as many of your favorites as you can.

On the other hand, if there are many new concepts that are all top priority but can't reasonably co-exist, then you need to try several, perhaps many, combinations until you find the one that has the greatest combined benefit for your story.

Though this takes time and is labor intensive, it is well worth it in the end, for your story will not only be far richer, but will excite you more in the writing of it, and therefore your work will be filled with far more passion, and your writing will progress more quickly.

The best way to try many different combinations is to use good old-fashioned index cards. Put each concept you'd like to include on its own card. Then, just like playing Scrabble, keep rearranging them, trying different groupings until your find the one that is the best for you.

Finally, organize that grouping into a list of its story elements that you can easily reference as preparation for Step 9, where you will weave them into your original synopsis in an all-inclusive revision.

~ Step 9 ~

Your Inspired Plot

In Step 8 you made a list of all the new material you've created that you'd like to include in your novel to fill holes and fix inconsistencies. In this step, you'll weave those concepts into your existing synopsis to fashion an all-inclusive and enriched version.

The first thing to do is re-read your synopsis from Step 5 to re-familiarize yourself with your novel as you originally saw it. Then, look over your list of the new story elements to be added to the mix.

Begin with the notion you'd most enjoy seeing in your story and, scanning your synopsis from top to bottom, locate the best place or places to insert it so that it will seamlessly integrate into your existing material. When you know where it is going to show up, re-write just that section (or sections) of your synopsis to include it.

After each inclusion of new material, scan over the rest of your synopsis to see if the changes conflict with any other sections. If so, make any additional alterations required to resolve those conflicts.

Repeat this process for all the concepts you wish to weave into your evolving story. Some new material may slip right in. Other times you may have to scratch your head a bit to see how you can wedge it in there. At times, you may have to reword a section you've already rewritten to add another concept or two in the same place.

Don't spend too much time on your exact wording. This isn't the time to be literary. That will happen in the next step when we wrap up the Inspiration: Plot section so we can move into Inspiration: Characters.

If there are some things you just can't find a home for, fret not, for that just indicates they probably don't belong in the same story with all the others.

When you have woven in as many of your new ideas as you can (again, within reason, without head-busting, face palms or the gnashing of teeth) move on to Step 10 so we can wrap up inspiration for your plot and get on with your characters!

~ Step 10 ~

Smoothing Out the Bumps

In Step 9 you integrated all your new material into your existing synopsis to create an all-inclusive description of your story's world. In this step you'll move things around and reword them so that your revised synopsis reads like butter.

You've come a long way. And, you've just completed a lot of hard work messing around with intangible ideas. Time to get literary again for a refreshing break.

Your job in this step is to reread your synopsis as it stands, not for content but from the standpoint of word play. For a moment, put story aside and think about *how* things are said rather than *what* is said. See if you can come up with a more interesting way to express the very same thing.

Don't feel you have to get too stylistic or come up with memorable ways of phrasing things – brilliant lines of soaring prose that sweep the reader off their mundane little feet.

Nobody is going to see this final plot revision but you. The purpose is not yet to create a finished work. Rather, you just want to iron out the wrinkles, trim the jagged edges, and smooth out the bumps for a pleasant flowing read.

So, crank open the stop-cocks of verbiage and pave a way through the telling of your story.

In Step 11, we'll fluff up your newly washed and folded story synopsis and see if we can shake some characters out of it.

Inspiration

Part Two: Characters

~ Step 11 ~

Who's There?

Congratulations! You've completed the first part of your journey toward a completed novel. It was a heck of a lot of work, but it is all about to pay off.

From here on out, we'll be drawing on material you've already created. What's more, each step from this point forward is far less complicated, requires far less effort and is shorter to boot!

In this step, for example, we're going to look for characters in the material you've already created. You don't have to invent anything new. In fact, it is important that you don't!

Read through your revised synopsis from Step 10 while asking yourself "who's there?" Make a list of all the characters *explicitly* called for in your story, as it is worded.

To be clear, don't list any characters you have in mind but didn't actually spell out in your work – just the ones who actually appear in the text.

You may have given some of these characters names. Others, you may have described simply by their roles in the story, such as Mercenary, John's Wife, Village Idiot, etc.

If a character does not yet have a role, give them one as a placeholder that more or less describes what they do, who they are related to, or what their situation is.

If a character does not yet have a name, don't hold yourself up trying to think of one now. Well have a whole step devoted to inventing interesting character names down the line.

For now, just list the characters actually spelled out specifically in your synopsis as it stands.

Example:

John - The Mercenary
An Archeologist
Painless Pete - A Dentist
A Clown
A Freelance Birdwatcher

Do NOT include any characters you have in mind but didn't actually mention. Do NOT include any characters who may be inferred but aren't actually identified. All those other characters will be dealt with in the next few steps.

So, get on with it and answer the burning question, "Who's There?"

~ Step 12 ~

Expected Characters

In Step 10 you made a list of all the characters explicitly named in your revised synopsis. Now list all the characters that your synopsis doesn't specifically name, but that would almost be expected in such a story. Include any additional characters you intend to employ but didn't actually spell out in your synopsis. Again, list them by role and name if one comes to mind.

Example:

Suppose a story is described as the tribulations of a town Marshall trying to fend off a gang of outlaws who bleed the town dry.

The only specifically called for characters are the Marshall and the gang, which you would have listed in Step 10. But, you'd also expect the gang to have a leader and the town to have a mayor. The Marshall might have a deputy. And, if the town is being bled dry, then some businessmen and shopkeepers would be in order as well.

So, you would list these additional *implied* characters as:

Gang Leader
Mayor
Deputy (John Justice)
Businessmen
Shopkeepers

Don't list every character you can possibly imagine – we'll expand our cast in other areas in steps to come. The task here is no more than to list all those characters most strongly implied – the ones that the plot or situation virtually calls for but doesn't actually name.

Add these new characters below those in you listed in Step 10. Then, in the next step we'll add some more!

~ Step 13 ~

The Usual Characters

In the previous step, you added characters implied by your synopsis to your potential cast list. Range a little wider now, and jot down some characters that aren't explicitly mentioned or even implied but wouldn't seem particularly out of place in such a story.

Example:

In the example story we've been using, no one would be surprised at all to encounter a saloon girl, a bartender, blacksmith, rancher, preacher, schoolteacher, etc.

There is no specific limit to how many or how few "usual characters" you can or should add to your growing cast list. So just add the ones that appeal to you.

Don't be worried if any of your additions seem stereotypical of too predictable. By the time we're through a few more steps your list will be so large we'll need to pare it down.

So for now, beef up your cast with any additional characters that would fit right in your novel as described in your synopsis.

~ Step 14 ~

Unusual Characters

In the previous step you added to your cast list some characters who would not raise an eyebrow if they showed up in your story's world.

Now, let yourself go a bit (but just a bit) and list a number of characters that might seem somewhat out of place but would still be fairly easily explainable in such a story as yours.

Example:

In our example story of a small town in the old west, these "unusual characters" might include:

A troupe of traveling acrobats
Ulysses S. Grant
A Prussian Duke
A bird watcher

You may be wondering why you'd want to have such odd characters in an otherwise normal story. The reason is to prevent your story from being *too* normal.

Neither reader nor publisher will want to waste time or money on a book that is just a rehash of the same tired material they've read over and over again.

What they are looking for is something with a unique personality – something that sets itself apart from the usual run of the mill.

Adding one or two somewhat unexpected characters to a story can liven up the cast and make it seem original, rather than derivative.

Once again, you won't be married to all these characters. They are just a gene pool from which to select your actual cast in a later step.

So, add to your list some slightly odd, offbeat, unexpected or quirky characters – no one too unusual, mind you – just folks who would not immediately come to mind in a story such as yours but could be explained with a little effort – folks to add a little color and interest to your story.

In the next step we'll pull out all the stops!

~ Step 15 ~

Outlandish Characters

In the last step you added some unusual characters to your story, but not so unusual that they couldn't easily be explained.

In this step we'll pull out all the stops and list some completely inappropriate characters that would take a heap of explaining to your readers if they showed up in your story.

Example:

In our example story set in an old western town, such characters might be:

Richard Nixon
Martians
Ghost of Julius Caesar

Pretty "out there," right? Although you'll likely discard these characters in our pruning step down the line, the process of coming up with outlandish characters can lead to new ideas and directions for your story.

For example, the town Marshall might become more interesting if he was a history buff, specifically reading about the Roman Empire. In his first run-in with the gang, he is knocked out cold with a concussion. For the rest of the story, he keeps imagining the Ghost of Julius Caesar, giving him unwanted advice.

Now's the time to let you Muse run wild and drag some truly outlandish characters into your story. Don't hold back, you can always axe them later, but you might just discover the most memorable character you've ever created and perhaps a truly original way to use them as well.

In the next step, we'll begin the process of transforming your characters, even the outlandish ones, into real people, preliminary to deciding which ones stay and which ones go.

~ Step 16 ~

What's in a Name?

In the last step you added some truly outlandish characters to your growing potential cast. Now in this step, you'll interview all the folks that showed up to be in your story to learn a bit more about them, to help you decide who to hire.

You're going to be collecting a lot of information about each of your characters individually, so either make a list, open up a spreadsheet, or just grab a few good ol' index cards to help you keep everything straight.

(Note: You probably won't end up using all the characters you've created so far. But we want to keep them all for now so you can scavenge some of their traits later to spice up the other characters you ultimately select as your cast.)

The first step in any interview is to get to get the character's name. You probably already have names of many of your potential cast members, but there are likely to be a few whose names you don't yet know.

For the nameless ones, it's time to give them a moniker. Names give us our first impression of a character. In most stories you'll want to keep most of your characters' names normal and simple. But if they are too normal or if everyone has an ordinary name, you're just boring your readers.

However, if your story *requires* typical names, try to pick ones that don't sound like one another or your readers may become confused as to which one you are talking about. Personally, I've always had trouble remembering which one is Sauron and which is Sarumon, but that's just me. Nonetheless, stay away from character combos like Jeanne and Jenny, Sonny and Sammy, Bart And Bret and – well, you get the idea.

If your story might benefit from giving some of your characters more unusual names, consider nicknames. Nicknames are wonderful dramatic devices because they can work with the character's apparent nature, against it for humiliating or comedic effect, play into the plot by telegraphing the activities in which the character will engage, create irony, or provide mystery by hinting at information or a backstory for the character that led to its nickname but has not yet been divulged to the readers.

Keep in mind these are just temporary names for identification. You'll have the chance to change them later. So for now, just add a name to every character in your potential cast list.

~ Step 17 ~

Gender Specific

For every character you are going to want to check the gender box on their interview sheet: Male, Female or Undecided.

Most characters will have an obvious gender, though some (like a shark or the wind) might be neuter or indeterminate. Usually, a gender helps the reader know how to relate to a character, as it is one of the first things humans instinctively try to determine, right after *friend* or *foe*.

Gender alters our entire sense of a person, critter or entity, so note one for every character in your list, if you can. Don't overthink the plumbing, as it were. For now, just go with the obvious choice and we'll mix things up a bit later on.

~ Step 18 ~

The Reason of Age

How old your characters are couches them in a lot of preconceptions about how they'll act, what their experience base is, and how formidable or capable they may be at the tasks that are thrust upon them in your story and even how they will relate to one another.

Many authors, especially those working on their first novel, tend to create characters who are all about the same age as the author.

This makes some sense insofar as a person can best write about that with which they are most familiar. The drawback is that anyone in your potential readership who falls outside your age range won't find anyone in your novel to whom they can easily relate. So, unless you are specifically creating your novel for a particular consistent age range, try to mix it up a bit and at least sprinkle your cast with folks noticeably older and younger than yourself.

Consider these issues while assigning an age to each character in your list.

~ Step 19 ~

Other Attributes

Like real people, your characters will have a wide range of other attributes, such as the religion to which they subscribe, special skills like horseback riding or a good singing voice, physical traits, such as being overweight, their race, abilities/disabilities or a nervous tick, mental attributes including IQ, savantism or autism, and hobbies or other interests like coin collecting or memorizing movie quotes.

Most of these attributes will amount to no more than window dressing in your story, but some of them may ultimately affect its course, and key events in your plot and/or message may hinge on a few of them.

There's no *absolute* need at this point to add any of these to each character's interview sheet – we'll revisit this kind of material later in the development stage – so don't go off into the woods on this one.

Still, if any additional attributes come to mind while interviewing your characters, jot them down as they will enrich your character and make them far more human and accessible to your readers.

~ Step 20 ~

Swap Meet

In the last step you made sure each of your potential characters had a vocation, name, gender, age and perhaps additional personal attributes.

In this step we're going to swap around some of those traits to make your list of potential characters even more original, interesting and memorable than before.

Our creative minds tend to fall into the same patterns over and over again. As a result, our characters run the risk of becoming overused stereotypes. By exchanging traits, we can create characters that transcend our inspirational ruts and become far more interesting and memorable.

Don't feel pressured to alter the original collection of attributes you had assigned to any given character if you are truly happy and comfortable with it. Still, mixing things up a bit just to see what happens can't hurt and just might just turn out to build an even more intriguing character.

Task One: Swapping Jobs

In this section rearrange your characters' jobs until you have created a new cast list with all the same information except different vocations for each.

For example, a Mercenary named Killer and a Seamstress named Jane are inherently less interesting that Seamstress named Killer and a Mercenary named Jane.

Swap jobs around a few times, locking in the combinations you like and reverting to the original arrangement of attributes for those you don't. Then, move on to Task Two….

Task Two: Swapping Genders

Every culture has preconceptions of the kinds of vocations appropriate to each sex. Adhering to these expectations makes characters familiar but also makes them predictable and ordinary.

By changing the gender of at least some of your less interesting characters, you can breathe new life into them.

For example, a male Mercenary is typical, a female Mercenary is not. A character called "John's Wife" does not necessarily have to be female, especially in this day and age.

Referring to your revised cast list including the new vocations, swap gender assignments among your characters to create even more interesting cominbations.

Task Three: Swapping Ages

We tend to write about characters our own age, or to assume a particular age by virtue of vocation. For example, an action character such as a Bush Pilot, or Spy is usually set as ranging between 25 and 50. An elementary school student is usually 5 to 12.

But what if you had a Bush Pilot in the range of 5 to 12 and an elementary school student of 25 to 50? In fact, these characters are not only more interesting, but easier to write, simply because the contrasts they express spur all kinds of creative inspirations.

Referring to your newly revised cast list from Task Two, swap the ages around to create a new list with these additional changes.

Task Four: Swapping Additional Attributes

Just as you have done with jobs, genders and ages, swap around any additional attributes you may have assigned to your characters to see if they make your potential cast members even more interesting.

When you have settled on the best possible combinations of attributes for each character, move on to the next step to audition these people for a role in your novel.

~ Step 21 ~

Auditioning Your Cast

Now that you have mixed things up a bit with your potential characters, there is one last task to do before selecting which ones to hire for your novel: the audition!

Each character is currently just a collection of traits – the parts with no sum. To know how each might play in your story, you need to get a more organic sense of them. In other words, you need to get to know them as people, not just as statistics.

To do this, have each of your potential cast members write a short paragraph about themself in their own words, describing themself, their attitudes, outlooks on life and incorporating all the attributes you've assigned to them.

Try to write these paragraphs in the unique *voice* of each character and from their point of view. Don't write about them; let them write about themselves.

This will give you the experience of what it is like to see the world through each character's eyes, which will help you understand their motivations and also make it easier for you to write your novel in such a way that your readers can step into your characters' shoes.

In the next step, you'll use these auditions to pare down your potential cast members to those who really belong in your novel.

~ Step 22 ~

Character Point Of View (POV)

Now that you know something about the personalities of your potential cast members, it is time to find out how they see your story.

In this step, you'll have each character write another paragraph from their point of view, but this time describing the basic plot of your story as it appear to them.

This will make your story more realistic by helping you understand and describe how each character sees and feels about the events unfolding around them.

Some characters may be integral to the plot. Others may simply be interesting folk who populate your story's world. Be sure each character includes how they see their role (if any) in the events, or if they seem themselves as just an observer or bystander. If they *are* involved in the plot, outline the nature of their participation as they see it.

Again, you don't want to go into great detail at this time. What you want is just an idea of how your story looks through each character's eyes. This will help you later on not only to decide which characters you want in your story, but how you might employ them as well.

In the next step we'll get to know your characters even better by investigating any personal and/or moral issues with which they grapple.

~ Step 23 ~

Personal Issues

We all have personal issues – trouble with co-workers, family difficulties, unfulfilled hopes or dreams or a moral dilemma.

Though it is not necessary, every character can benefit from having a personal issue with which it must grapple or a belief system that comes under attack.

A moral dilemma, worldview or philosophy of life helps your characters come off as real people, rather than just functional players in the story. In addition, readers identify more easily with characters that have an internal struggle, and care about them more as well.

Consider each of your potential cast members, one by one. Read their entire dossier so far consisting of their list of attributes, self-description and perspective on your story.

If a belief system, personal code of behavior, philosophy, worldview, moral outlook or internal conflict is indicated, note it and write a few words about it in their dossier. If a character has emotional issues regarding themselves, their world or the people in it, note that as well.

If you don't see such an issue already present, read between the lies to see if one is inferred. If so, write a few words about that.

Now don't beat your head against the wall looking for something that may not be there. If a personal issue isn't indicated, it makes no sense to try to impose one. Some characters are better off without them.

For this step, just look over what you already know about each character and then single out and describe any personal issues it might have.

~ Step 24 ~

Selecting Your Cast

Congratulations! Over the last few steps you've learned a tremendous amount of information about your characters' attributes, self-image, outlook, and personal issues.

With all the work you've done, you probably have more characters than you need or want. Still, by keeping them around, you have had the opportunity to inject new blood into old stereotypes. As a result, your potential cast represents a healthy mix of interesting people.

The task at hand is to pare down this list by selecting only those characters you really want or actually need in your story.

To begin, make three categories, either as columns on a page or piles of index cards: one for obvious rejects, one for *maybes*, and one for the characters you are absolutely certain you want in your novel.

Put into the *Keeper* pile every character that is essential to your plot, contributes extraordinary passion, or is just so original and intriguing you can wait to write about them.

In the *Not Sure* pile, place all the characters who have some function (though they aren't the only one who could perform it), have some passionate contribution (but it seems more peripheral than central), or are mildly interesting but not all-consuming fascinating.

In the *No Way!* Pile, place all the characters who don't have a function, don't contribute to the passionate side of your story and rub you the wrong way.

After distributing all your characters into these three categories, leaf through the "maybe" category, character by character, to see if any of them would fit will and without redundancy in the cast you've already selected.

If any would uniquely bring something worthwhile to your story that couldn't be contributed by a keeper character, add them to your cast for now. If they would not, add them to the rejects.

Finally, look through the rejects for any individual attributes that you are sorry to see go – character traits you'd like to explore in your novel, even if you are sure you don't want the whole character.

If there are any, distribute those attributes among your chosen characters as long as they don't conflict with or lessen their existing quality and power. In this way, you will infuse your cast with the most potent elements possible.

You now have your initial cast of characters for your novel. In the actual writing to come, you may determine that certain characters are not playing out as well as expected. At that time, you can always cut them from your cast and redistribute any desirable attributes among your other characters.

Or, you may discover there are some essential jobs left undone, and you'll need to create one or more additional characters to fill that gap.

But, for now, you have finally arrived at your initial cast – the folks who will populate your story's world, drive the action, consider the issues, and involve your readers.

In the next step, we'll explore the nature of your Main Character before turning our attention to your story's theme.

~ Step 25 ~

Your Main Character

Of all your cast, there is one very special player: the Main Character. Your Main Character is the one your story seems to be about – the one with whom your readers most identify – in short, the single most important character in your novel.

You probably already know who your Main Character is. If, so, you'll find this step opens opportunities to avoid stereotyping him or her. If you haven't yet selected your Main Character, this step will help you choose one from your cast list.

First, your Main Character is not necessarily your protagonist. While the protagonist is the prime mover of the effort to achieve the story goal, the Main Character is the one who grapples with an inner dilemma, personal issue or has some aspect of his or her belief system come under attack.

Most writers combine these two functions into a single player (a hero) who is both protagonist *and* Main Character in order to position their readers right at the heart of the action, as in the Harry Potter series.

Still, there are good reasons for not always blending the two. In the book and movie *To Kill A Mockingbird*, the protagonist is Atticus – a southern lawyer trying to acquit a young black man wrongly accused of rape. That is the basic plot of the story.

But the Main Character is Atticus' young daughter, Scout. While the overall story is about the trial, that is really just a background to Scout's experiences as we see prejudice through her eyes – a child's eyes.

??!

In this way, the author (Dee Harper) distances us from the incorruptible Atticus so that we do not feel all self-righteous. And, by making Scout effectively prejudiced against Boo Radley (the scary "boogie man" who lives down the street), we see how easily we can all become prejudiced by fearing what we really know nothing about.

In the end, Boo turns out to be Scout's secret protector, and the story's message about both the evils and ease of prejudice is made.

Your story may be best suited to center around a typical hero, especially if it is an action story or physical journey story. But if you are writing more of an exploration novel in which the plot unfolds as a background against which a personal journey of self-discovery or a resolution of personal demons is told, then separating your Main Character from the protagonist (and the heart of the action) may serve you better.

Armed with this understanding, review the cast you have chosen for your novel. If you have already selected a Main Character, see if they are a hero who is also the protagonist, driving the action. If so, consider splitting those functions into two players to see if it might enhance your story for your readers. If you have already set up a separate Main Character and protagonist, consider combining them into a hero, to see if that might streamline your story.

If you have not yet chosen a Main Character and/or a protagonist, review your cast list to see if one player would best do both jobs or if one would better drive the plot and the other would better carry the message.

When you have made your choices, write a brief paragraph about your Main Character and/or protagonist to explain how those two functions are satisfied by your chosen character or characters.

~ Step 26 ~

Revised Synopsis

Now that you have selected a variety of intriguing characters as your cast and chosen your Main Character and protagonist, it is time to revise your overall story synopsis to weave this material into your story.

Referring to your most recently revised synopsis from Step 10, note all the places you have previous mentioned characters.

If any of the characters already in your synopsis no longer exist in your cast, either replace them with characters who do and can perform the same job or eliminate whatever mention there was and pull up your text so it doesn't leave a conceptual hole.

Then, begin with the character in your cast of whom you are most enamored and integrate it into your story wherever you think he or she would enrich your story. One by one, add in the others.

You don't need to work in everything you've learned about each character – much of that material can serve better as background for your own use when you get down to the actual business of writing.

Rather, draw on each character's dossier for material that can become part of your plot, the basis for character relationships to be developed in later steps, and for your story's theme, moral or message.

Once you have blended your characters into your synopsis as fully as you can, read it over from stem to stern and refine it into a polish draft that reads smoothly.

Again, no need to be particularly literary in style. Just ensure there are no holes, inconsistencies or areas of confusion due to wording.

In our next step we'll leave characters behind and find inspiration for your story's theme.

Inspiration

Part Three:
Theme

~ Step 27 ~

Thematic Topic

Many authors don't have a theme in mind when the come to a story. They are often more interested in the genre, setting, action, or characters. But without a theme to glue the pieces together, a story seems to meander aimlessly, not covering specific ground but just heading off in any direction.

The theme has two parts:

1. The topic of the story.
2. The moral or message of the story.

The topic is the broad subject area explored, which may be material or conceptual. Death, the complexity of society, nuclear power or man's inhumanity to man are all potent thematic topics.

In contrast, the moral or message of a story explores an individual human quality such as greed, self-sacrifice, conceit or compassion.

In this step, we'll locate and refine your thematic topic. Then, in a few more steps, we'll do the same for your story's message.

To begin, read through your most recent synopsis with an eye toward any overarching topics addressed in it. If you see one or more unifying topics, list them.

If you don't see an overarching topic already in your story, you are going to need one. Re-read your existing synopsis and look for smaller mentions of topical subject matter that is of personal interest to you as an author or one of your characters, even if it is barely mentioned or exists only between the lines, and put these topics in a list.

Once you have your topic list, write a few words about each: why they interest you, how you feel about them, why you believe they are important.

Now it's time to select the central topic of your story. You may find that your list contains one particular topic of such great interest to you that the choice is easy.

Or, you may find that none of the topics outshines the rest. If you can't choose one, consider whether some of your potential topics might actually be sub-categories of one or more of the other topics. If they are, the parent topic would be the one to choose, with the others being part of its exploration.

If you are still baffled, consider the events in your plot and the kinds of characters in your story. Which of the topics in the list are most likely to be covered in the course of your characters engaging in their plot activities?

Choosing the topic your characters and plot will most often touch upon is a good means of coalescing your story around your theme.

When you have selected the principal topic you'd like to address in your story, move on to the next step where we will create specific story instances that illustrate and explore your thematic topic.

~ Step 28 ~

Topic Illustrations

To fully explore a thematic topic, several examples of the topic must appear in your story. For instance, if the topic were Death, then the central example might be the slow demise of a loved one of the Main Character over the course of the story.

Other supporting instances in the same story would be plants withering in the window boxes around town due to a drought, a still-born puppy, or the closing of a family-run business that has been around for over a century.

To begin, list a primary or central example of your thematic topic, either drawn from your synopsis or newly created with a mind to your plot and characters.

Then list as many subordinate examples as readily come to mind. Not to worry if you have trouble coming up with very many. As you continue to develop your story, opportunities to express your thematic topic often suggest themselves.

~ Step 29 ~

Thematic Message

Your thematic message will explore a particular human quality such as greed, denial, or living in fantasy. The message need not be about something bad, but could be about the value of a positive quality.

The Main Character is the focus of the thematic message, as when greed is explored through Scrooge in "A Christmas Carol."

In Step 23 you gave each of your characters a personal issue that plagues them in the story. In Step 25, you chose one of these players as your Main Character. Referring to your Main Character's personal issue, describe the human quality at the heart of his or her dilemma. Then, expand on that description so that quality becomes the subject of your story's overall message as well.

If you are not satisfied with the way that human quality develops as a message, go back and re-envision your Main Character's personal dilemma accordingly until you find a shading of it that also works as the subject of the message as well.

In the next step, we'll create a number of specific events or situations that will illustrate your novel's thematic message throughout the story.

~ Step 30 ~

Message Illustrations

To make your thematic point, you'll need to convince your readers that what you have to say about the moral issue is true. To do this, you'll need a number of instances in which that human quality is shown to be a positive or negative thing.

Although your story's message centers on the Main Character who grapples with the issue at a personal level, many of your other characters may be used to illustrate the value or detriment of that quality as well.

Consider all your characters as potential harbingers when creating illustrations of your message, but try to make sure the strongest instances revolve around your Main Character.

As an example, consider *A Christmas Carol* by Charles Dickens. While Scrooge is certainly the center of the thematic argument regarding greed, he is not the only representative of that human quality.

Consider the other businessmen who will go to Scrooge's funeral "if a lunch is provided." Also of note are the greedy scavengers who steel Scrooge's drapes and sheets after he is dead. Then there are the moneylenders who shut down old Fezziwig's business. In fact, there are scores of illustrations of the thematic message in most every great novel.

Each illustration should be a little scene in itself. It doesn't have to be long or complex, but it does need to be a little self-contained moment that encapsulates and crystallizes an instance of your message, even if that moment is just a beat in a larger event.

So, design as many instances as is reasonably fun and comfortable, and in the next step, we'll weave all of the thematic material you've developed so far into your revised synopsis.

~ Step 31 ~

Revised Synopsis

Now that you have developed a thematic topic and message issue and (hopefully) several if not many illustrations of each, it is time to work this material into your existing synopsis.

Revise your synopsis now to include all your thematic material and then polish it up for a smooth read.

Inspiration

Part Four:
Genre

~ Step 32 ~

Introduction

Many novice authors view Genre as a list of requirements or a box in which one must write. Stories created this way are usually predictable and formulaic.

A better way is to see Genre as the overall "feel" of the finished work. An author gives himself or herself the freedom to let the story grow in the directions it wants, without constraint. Then what makes the story feel more like a horror story or a western are the storytelling elements peppered into it along the way.

Not all genres rely on the same kinds of elements. Some genres, like Westerns, are based on a particular setting and often a particular time period. Others, like action stories are based on the kinds of events that take place. So, a Western like "High Noon" is not an action story, while a Western like "Shanghai Noon" is, thereby spanning two sub-genres.

Horror stories are about varieties of physical torment, Comedies are affecting the audience directly by making it laugh, regardless of setting, time period, or activities.

The point here is that one need not be confined to a single traditional genre. In fact, the more blending you do, the more original your novel will come to be.

In this step we'll begin the process of creating the unique feel of your novel by having you choose as many traditional genres that you might like to draw upon.

The following list covers a number of popular genres to get you started.

COMMON GENRES:

Western, Mystery, Horror, Comedy, Drama, Action, Romance, Musical, Biography, Thriller, Black Comedy, Situation Comedy, Comedy of Manners, Comedy of Errors, Tragedy, Period Drama, Historical, Epic, Science Fiction, Space Opera, Fantasy, Ethnic, War, Anti-War, Romantic Comedy, Spy, Heist, Spoof, Survival, True-to-life, Musical Comedy, Personal Growth, Relationships.

Now, write the names of all the different genres you might want to include elements of in your story. Example: Horror and Comedy are two of the genres used in the *Scary Movie* series of films.

~ Step 33 ~

Genre Elements

Each genre brings to mind certain essential or at least common ingredients. For example, the list of elements in the Western genre might include:

- Cowboys
- Horses
- Frontier Town
- Saloon
- Gunfight
- Stampede

Some of these elements are characters. Others are locations. Some are events.

The elements in other genres may include storytelling style (such as keeping the audience guessing in a mystery), references to other stories (as in a spoof), or the relationships among characters (as in a Buddy Story or Romantic Comedy).

By creating an extensive list of genre elements, you will have a wealth of options for adding detail and richness to the overall feel of your novel.

Referring to your chosen genres from the last step, describe the elements you would expect to find in each. List as many as you can.

~ Step 34 ~

Your Unique Genre

Referring to the collection of elements you gathered in the last step, use it as a shopping list, selecting only those elements from each genre you might like to include in your story.

By picking and choosing genre elements from several genres rather than adopting a complete set from a single genre, you will break out of formula and your story will seem far more fresh and original, even while still feeling familiar.

~ Step 35 ~

Revised Synopsis

Your list of genre elements currently stands by itself as components. The idea here is to make specific reference to these elements throughout your synopsis whenever you can.

By spelling out specifically how each of the elements you'd *like* to include actually *will* be included, you lay the groundwork for your novel's unique genre, not just a generic one.

Referring to your synopsis and your list of chosen genre elements, revise your synopsis to pepper it with as many those elements as you can.

~ Step 36 ~

Story Holes

Now that you have created a complete synopsis with elements of plot, characters, theme, and genre, it is time to stand back, look at the big picture, and see what holes may have worked their way into the fabric of your story.

Although you may want to take a stab at this now, it is often better to put your story aside for a day or two to gain some perspective. That way you avoid a typical author's problem of assuming you have included material that is really in between the lines or only in your own creative mind, not on paper!

When you are ready, put yourself in the reader position. Re-read your synopsis and then, using the Creativity Two-Step method, list below all of the questions that come to mind, based solely on what you have actually written.

When you can find no more holes, proceed to the next question.

~ Step 37 ~

Filling the Holes

Referring to the list of questions about your story you listed in the last step, come up with one or more potential answer for each if you can.

If you can't think of an answer to a given question, you've got a hole the audience will see too.

There are several things you can do about this:

1. Keep working to fill the hole.

2. Rather than add material to fill the hole, remove the material around the hole. (In this way, the question will never come up!)

3. Leave the hole because it isn't that bad and you don't want to remove the material around it.

Any and all of these approaches can work. Keep in mind that stories are about passion, not about structural holes. The only time holes are visible is when the storytelling isn't strong enough to gloss over them. So, if you can't figure out how to fill a hole and are confident of your ability to cover it up, no problem.

For this step then, follow the Creativity Two-Step approach and find as many answers as you can to the questions you asked in the last step.

~ Step 38 ~

Cramming It All In

In this step is a big job that require little explanation:

Re-write your existing synopsis in the space below to plug as many holes as possible by working in the answers you devised in the last step.

~ Step 39 ~

Polish Draft

In the last step, you have created a revised synopsis of your overall story including depth, richness and detail. Quite a bit more than you had when you started!

But, since each piece was added on top of existing work, the synopsis may seem a little bit like a patchwork quilt.

The task at hand is to smooth the edges and blend the pieces together until it feels as if the whole story idea must have been thought of in its entirety, rather than section at a time.

Again, you may want to put your story away for a day or so until your preconceptions fade enough to see the rough spots.

When you are satisfied with how your synopsis reads, you may want to share it with friends you trust to be honest but not to stab you in your creative heart.

Don't change anything just because one person felt strongly about it. But if you see a consistency among several people, it is worth reconsidering that point.

Armed with any comments you feel are valid, re-rewrite your synopsis until you are satisfied it reads easily and incorporates every improvement worth making.

At this point, congratulations are in order! With diligence commitment and a heck of a lot of work, you have completed the Inspiration Stage and are ready to move on to Stage Two: Story Development!

To begin, advance to the next page....

Development

Part One:
Plot

~ Step 40 ~

Story Goal

Some novice writers become so wrapped up in interesting events and bits of action that they forget to have a central unifying goal that gives purpose to all the other events that take place. This creates a plot without a core.

But determining your story's goal can be difficult, especially if your story is character oriented, and not really about a Grand Quest.

For example, in the movie "Four Weddings and a Funeral," all the characters are struggling with their relationships and not working toward an apparent common purpose. There is a goal, however, and it is to find happiness in a relationship.

This type of goal is called a "Collective Goal" since it is not about trying to achieve the same thing, but the same *kind* of thing.

So don't try to force some external, singular purpose on your story if it isn't appropriate. But do find the common purpose in which all your characters share a critical interest.

Referring to your story synopsis, have you included a Goal in which all the characters are involved?

If so, describe it below in as much detail as readily comes to mind.

If not, consider your subject matter and the activities in which your characters engage. What singular achievement would affect them all for better or worse?

~ Step 41 ~

Personal Goals

Personal Goals are the motivating reasons your characters care about and/or participate in the effort to achieve or prevent the overall goal. In other words, they see the main story goal as a means to an end, not as an end itself.

Although a personal goal for each character is not absolutely essential, at some point your readers are going to wonder what is driving each character to brave the trials and obstacles. If you haven't supplied a believable motivation, it will stand out as a story hole.

Referring to the descriptions you wrote about what your story would be like if told through the eyes of each of your characters and about their personal issues, describe what each of your characters might have for a personal goal that would lead them to participate in the effort to achieve the central story goal.

~ Step 42 ~

Requirements

The success or failure in achieving the goal is an important but short moment at the end of the story. So how is interest maintained over the course of the story? By the progress of the quest toward the goal. This progress is measured by how many of the requirements have been met and how many remain.

Requirements can be logistic, such as needing to obtain five lost rubies that fit in the idol and unlock the door to the treasure. Or, they can be passionate, such as needing to perform enough selfless acts to win the heart of the princess.

The important thing is that the requirements are clear enough to be easily understood and measurable enough to be "marked off the list" as the story progresses.

In this step, list the requirements that need to be met in order for the story's overall goal to be achieved.

~ Step 43 ~

Consequences

A goal is what the characters chase, but what chases the characters? The consequence doubles the dramatic tension in a story by providing a negative result if the goal is not achieved.

Consequences may be emotional or logistic, but the more intense they are, the greater the tension. Often it provides greater depth if there are emotional consequences when there is an external goal, and external consequences if there is an emotional goal.

Your novel might be about avoiding the consequences or it might begin with the consequences already in place, and the goal is intended to end them.

If the consequences are intense enough, it can help provide motivation for characters that have no specific personal goals.

In this step, describe the consequences that will occur if the characters in your story fail to achieve the story's goal.

~ Step 44 ~

Success or Failure?

A story without a clear indication of success or failure is a failure of a story. You need to work out exactly how your readers will know the goal is achieved or not.

This might seem obvious in an action story, but may be much more difficult in a story about character growth.

Success and Failure don't have to be binary choices; they can be matters of degree. For example, the effort to bring back a treasure may fail, but the adventurers discover one large ruby that fell into their pack. Or, someone seeking true love might find love but with someone who is rather annoying.

Whether either of these examples is a partial success or a partial failure depends largely on how you portray the characters' attitudes to the imperfect achievement.

In this step, state whether your story ends in success or failure, and how that is measured.

~ Step 45 ~

Plot Synopsis

Now that you have developed some key plot points, it's time to get an overview of your plot, independent of your story synopsis. This will help you look for holes and inconsistencies in the logistic spine of your novel.

Look back over your work on the plot elements of the last few steps and write a short synopsis describing how they work together in your plot

~ Step 46 ~

Revised Synopsis

Referring to your story synopsis and the plot synopsis you wrote in the last step, write a new story synopsis that incorporates the elements of both, blending your plot enhancements into your overall story.

Development

Part Two: Characters

~ Step 47 ~

Refine Your Protagonist

As described in Step 25 (The Main Character), the protagonist is one of the most misunderstood characters in a story's structure. It is often assumed that this character is a typical "Hero" who is a good guy, the central character, and the Main Character.

In fact, the protagonist does not have to be any of these things. By definition, the protagonist is the Prime Mover or Driver of the effort to achieve the goal. Beyond that, he, she, or it might be a bad guy (such as an anti-hero).

Being the central character just means that character is the most prominent to the audience. For example, Fagin in "Oliver Twist" is perhaps the most prominent, but he is certainly not the protagonist. So, a protagonist may actually be less interesting than the antagonist, or may even be almost a background character.

And as we have already explored, the Main Character is not always the protagonist, but could be any one of the characters in your novel who represents the reader position in the story.

So, the only attribute you should consider in refining your protagonist is to ensure this character is the one with the most initiative toward reaching the Goal.

Referring to your cast list, your plot synopsis and your story synopsis, confirm that the player you chose as your protagonist is still the best person for the job. If not, choose the player that is.

Then, taking into account all the plot elements you have added to your story in recent steps, write a short description of how your protagonist is crucially involved in your plot as its prime mover.

~ Step 48 ~

Your Antagonist

While the protagonist attempts to accomplish the goal, the antagonist seeks to thwart that effort, either preventing the achievement or by achieving it himself.

These efforts have nothing to do with whether the antagonist is a good guy or a bad guy. For example, in most James Bond films, the Villain is the protagonist, for it is he who initiates a plan, thereby driving the plot. Structurally, James Bond himself is an antagonist, since he tries to return things to the status quo.

So, who we cheer for and our moral prerogatives are really not involved in this choice.

Referring to your cast of characters, your plot synopsis and the refinement of your protagonist you wrote in the last step, pick one of your existing characters as your antagonist and describe how he, she, or it is focused on preventing the protagonist from achieving the story goal.

In the off chance that none of your characters can easily fulfill the role of antagonist, return to the character development steps and create a new character specifically for this task.

~ Step 49 ~

Protagonist Personal

Characters have dramatic functions, but the reader or audience needs to identify with them as real people. A necessary but difficult task is to intertwine the personal and structural aspects of each character so that they blend seamlessly together and become interdependent in a unified person.

For your protagonist, what personal qualities or previous experiences have led them to become a protagonist in this particular story, the Prime Mover in the effort to achieve the goal? Conversely, if your character by nature is wishy-washy, how does that affect their efforts when called upon by story circumstances to function as a protagonist?

By integrating all aspects of a character together, it will seem to be driven by real motivations, enacted in a truly human manner.

To further refine your protagonist, refer to the material you developed for that character including personal goal and moral issue. If your protagonist is also your Main Character, consider what you developed there as well.

For this step, write a brief description of your protagonist's overall nature, incorporating all of this material.

~ Step 50 ~

Antagonist Personal

Now that you have chosen an antagonist, refer to the material you developed for that character including personal goal and moral issue, just as you did in the last step for your protagonist. If your antagonist is also your Main Character (possible, but not a common combination), consider what you developed there as well.

Now, write a brief description of your antagonist's overall nature, incorporating all of this material. Pay particular attention to how their personal aspects tie into their motivation and function to thwart the protagonist's efforts.

~ Step 51 ~

Main Character View

If your Main Character is neither your protagonist nor antagonist, describe how this character views and feels about the two opponents who are grappling over the goal.

Since the Main Character represents the reader position in the story, its view of the struggle between protagonist and antagonist has a huge impact on how your reader will feel about it as well.

~ Step 52 ~

Revised Synopsis

Now that you know which characters are your protagonist, antagonist and Main Character, and something about them as people, it is important to tie them in with the overall plot, which personalizes the events of the story. Otherwise, a plot comes off as dry and un-involving.

Referring to your most recent synopsis, revise the material to integrate what you have developed for your protagonist and antagonist, and Main Character.

~ Step 53 ~

Structural Roles

You've already chosen a protagonist and an antagonist, but those are not the only structural roles you can assign to your characters. In the hero's journey there are structural archetypes such as The Mentor, The Threshold Guardian, The Herald, The Shapeshifter, The Shadow, and The Trickster. Other Archetypes include the Sidekick, the Skeptic, the Love Interest, the Sage, the Fool, the Caregiver, Reason, Emotion, and many, many more.

Don't be worried that giving a character an archetypal role will diminish its humanity and make it stilted or stereotypical.

Selecting an archetypal role for each character gives that character a center and an important dramatic function in the story, rather that being there for entertainment only.

For more information on Archetypes, search the web for "Hero's Journey," "Joseph Campbell Archetypes," "Carl Jung Archetypes," "Dramatica Archetypes," etc. Or, read Joseph Campbell's *The Hero with a Thousand Faces*, Chris Vogler's "The Hero's Journey," or *Dramatica: A New Theory of Story*.

For this step, review your cast of characters and if possible, select an archetypal role for each. List each character, the archetypal role you are assigning to it, and a brief description of how that role pertains to its actions in your plot (referring to your story synopsis).

~ Step 54 ~

Situational Relationships

While archetypal functions describe a character's attitude and/or approach in the plot, situational relationships describe how characters interact in their environment.

Some of these relationships are based on blood or marriage, such as brother or sister, husband, wife, uncle, etc. Others are based on job relationships, such as police captain and beat cop, boss and employee, or student and teacher. Still others are based on common interests such as membership in the same club or in competing clubs, going to the same or a different church, and so on.

Although situational relationships are not essential, they add a whole layer of interactive complexity to your characters and plot, making your story much more like real life.

For this step, write a brief description for each character of all the situational relationships they have with other characters.

~ Step 55 ~

Emotional Relationships

Regardless of whether or not your characters have structural or situational relationships, they will have feelings about each other.

There are no rules about who should like, dislike, respect, fear, or love whom. Such choices are part of the intuitive art of storytelling. The one sure thing is that instilling feelings in each of your characters about the others will give them humanity and involve your readers emotionally in your story.

For each of your characters, describe any emotional relationships they have with your other characters. Keep in mind that feelings do not have to be mutual.

~ Step 56 ~

Relationships Synopsis

Referring to the material you have just developed for your characters (including structural roles, structural relationships, situational relationships, and emotional relationships) incorporate all of this information into an overall synopsis describing all the relationships among your characters.

~ Step 57 ~

Revised Story Synopsis

Referring to your existing synopsis for your story as a whole, rework the material to incorporate what you have developed in your Character Relationships Synopsis in the last step.

Development

Part Three: Theme

~ Step 58 ~

Counterpoint

For every human quality, there is the opposite quality. For example, greed is balanced by generosity, denial is balanced by acceptance, and living in fantasy is balanced by remaining grounded in fact.

What is the counterpoint to the message issue you selected? List it and write a brief description of how it is opposite to your message issue.

~ Step 59 ~

Counterpoint Illustrations

The Main Character will usually only exhibit the thematic topic, not the counterpoint, as the story's message revolves around whether the main character changes his ways or not.

In contrast, the counterpoint must be equally represented through your other characters to avoid making a one-sided moral argument. It is the comparison between the two that develops a thematic conflict that holds your readers' interest.

For this step, list as many scenarios as you can easily devise in which other characters employ the counterpoint quality. Later, we'll work them into a balanced thematic argument.

~ Step 60 ~

Thematic Conclusion

At the end of the story, there is usually one moment at which the author makes his or her own statement about which is the better side of the thematic conflict.

This moment should not be an attempt to prove which is better, as the proof has been already created by the balance between them in the ongoing examples over the course of the story. Rather, this is the time the author confirms the conclusions the audience has drawn for itself by showing how those characters who favored one side of the conflict ultimately fare against the characters who favored the other.

Referring to your story synopsis and what you have developed already for your theme, devise an event or situation for the end of your story that will provide a conclusion to the thematic conflict by confirming whether the message or counterpoint came out on top.

~ Step 61 ~

Revised Synopsis

Time to blend your enhanced thematic argument into your evolving novel. For this step, revise your existing story synopsis to incorporate the material you have recently developed for your counterpoint and thematic conclusion.

Development

Part Four:
Genre

~ Step 62 ~

Genre and Plot

Because genre permeates all aspects of a novel, it is best appreciated in combination with your plot, characters and theme.

Accordingly, this first section of Genre Development focuses on genre and plot. Plot is about the progression of events in your story. So, elements of genre that are about events like a car chase, a series of murders, or a first kiss are also a part of your plot as well.

In this step, the task is to incorporate into your plot as many of the genre elements you have previously selected in an earlier step.

Look through your list of genre elements. Consider which ones might have an impact the events and progression of your plot. Then, write a short description of the plot impact of each of those elements.

Limit yourself to plot only for this step. Character and Theme will be explored in the screens that follow.

Example: Suppose you are writing a Western and that one of your genre elements is brawl in the saloon. And, suppose your story synopsis calls for an argument between the Main Character (a cowboy) and his sister (a bar maid at the saloon). Even though your story synopsis did not call for a brawl, you can work that element into your plot by having the argument between the cowboy and his sister escalate into a knock-down, drag-out fight involving everyone in the saloon.

By "trying out" each genre element against the existing events of your synopsis, you may find all kinds of interesting juxtapositions that greatly enhance the interest-value of your story, even though you did not original intend such a turn of events.

There is no fixed number of genre elements that are required to be worked into a novel, but they are like spices in a meal – too few and it is bland, too many an it is obnoxious, just the right mix and it is a gourmet dish.

So, pepper your plot liberally with genre to spice it up, but don't overpower it.

~ Step 63 ~

Genre and Characters

Elements of genre may affect character relationships (as in a Comedy of Errors), attitudes (as in a Comedy of Manners), dialogue (in an Historical Drama), and much more.

Referring to your existing story synopsis and your list of genre elements, describe how specific genre elements affect your characters.

Limit yourself to characters only for this step. Theme will be explored in the step that follows.

~ Step 64 ~

Genre and Theme

Elements of genre may affect subject matter (as in a Spy Thriller), message (such as blind devotion to duty), counterpoint (questioning orders from a superior), and much more.

Referring to your existing story synopsis and your list of genre elements, describe as many specific instances as you can for every genre element that might affect your theme.

~ Step 65 ~

Revised Synopsis

Revise your existing story synopsis to incorporate the material you have just developed for your genre elements and their integration into your plot, characters, and theme.

Exposition

Part One:
Plot

~ Step 66 ~

Goal

Now that you have enriched your novel with additional development of your plot, characters, theme and genre, we're going to shift gears and consider how that information will be revealed to your readers.

Just because you know these things about your story doesn't mean your readers will as a result of what you write. One of the easiest mistakes to make, especially for first time novelists, is to write without an exposition plan, simply trying to tell the story.

While this is a very free form and organic way to get your novel told, you are likely to leave out important information because you are so familiar with it that you don't think to specifically include it.

So in this step, we'll begin the process of ensuring that all the essential information you know about your novel is conveyed to your readers, starting with your story's goal.

Sometimes the goal is spelled out right at the beginning, such as a meeting in which a general tells a special strike unit that a senator's daughter has been kidnapped by terrorists and they must rescue her.

Other times, the goal is hidden behind an apparent goal. So, if your story had used the scene described above, it might turn out that was really just a cover story and in fact, the supposed "daughter" was actually an agent who was assigned to identify and kill a double agent working in the strike team.

Goals may also be revealed slowly, such as in "The Godfather," where it takes the entire film to realize the goal is to keep the mob organization alive by replacing the aging Don with a younger member of the family.

Further, in "The Godfather," as in many Alfred Hitchcock films, the goal is not nearly as important as the chase or the inside information or the thematic atmosphere. So don't feel obligated to elevate every story point to the same level.

As long as each key story point is there in some way, to some degree of importance, there will be no story hole. Still, you may have a lot of interest in a particular story point. A character's personal goal, for example, may touch on an issue that you want to explore in greater detail.

When this is the case, let your imagination run wild. Jot down as many instances as come to mind in which the particular plot point comes into play. Such events, moments, or scenarios enrich a story and add passion to a perfunctory telling of the tale.

One of the best ways to do this is to consider how each plot point might affect other plot points, and other story points pertaining to characters, theme, and genre.

For example, each character sees the overall goal as a step in helping them accomplish their personal goals. So, why not create a scenario where a character wistfully describes his personal goal to another character while sitting around a campfire? He can explain how achievement of the overall story goal will help him get what he personally wants.

An example of this is in the John Wayne classic movie, "The Searchers." John Wayne's character asks an old, mentally slow friend to help search for the missing girl. Finding the girl is the overall goal. The friend has a personal goal - he tells Wayne that he just wants a roof over his head and a rocking chair by the fire. This character sees his participation in the effort to achieve the goal as the means of obtaining something he has personally longed for.

And how does your story goal exemplify or affect the moral or message of your story as part of the theme? When you see the story goal mentioned in your story synopsis, determine if you can incorporate aspects of theme, and when you see theme, try to add a reference to the goal.

In "Huckleberry Finn," Mark Twain has the boy cooking up some food for Tom Sawyer. He puts all the vegetables and meat in the same pan and explain that his pop taught him that food is better when the flavors all "swap around" a bit.

The same is true for stories. Don't speak just about goal, speak about goal in reference to as many other story points as you can.

Your task for this step - first describe how you will reveal the goal to your readers so you are sure you've at least covered that base. Then, describe as many other scenarios as you can where goal impacts, influences, or affects other story points to reinforce it in your readers' minds.

~ Step 67 ~

Personal Goals

Earlier, you developed personal goals for each of your characters. At a personal level, the main Story Goal may be seen by them as just the means to an end of accomplishing their own goals.

In this step, describe how you let your readers learn the nature of each character's personal goal.

Don't forget to jot down any additional instances that come to mind where characters' personal goals come into play after they have been revealed.

Especially consider creating scenarios in which you can fold other story points into the same event, moment, or conversation.

~ Step 68 ~

Requirements

The easiest way to reveal your goal's requirements is to come right out and say it, such as "You must recover the five holy stones of the idol to seal the dimensional rift." Of course, there are more interesting indirect ways as well.

The nature of each next requirement might be provided only after the current requirement is met. This works like game where each clue that is found indicates the location of the next clue until the final destination is reached.

Sometimes, the requirements appear arbitrary until enough of them are met and then a pattern begins to emerge, indicating all that still remain to be completed.

No matter how you reveal your requirements, make sure your readers are ultimately clear on exactly what is required of your characters or your story will seem arbitrary.

Once you have revealed the requirements, however, they still need to be met. This will likely involve some effort on the part of your characters. The more difficulty the characters have - the more obstacles in their way - the more dramatic tension builds in your readers. To take advantage of this, try making each Requirement a miniature Goal, with its own sub-requirements.

Now, describe how you will reveal what the requirements are, then list as many different scenarios as you can in which each requirement comes into play and is met, especially in conjunction with other story points.

~ Step 69 ~

Consequences

In most stories, the Consequence is what will happen if the Goal is not achieved. In some stories, however, the Consequence already exists, and will continue to be suffered unless or until the Goal is achieved. Either way, for maximum tension in your novel, you need to ensure your readers are clear on what will happen if the effort to achieve the goal end in failure.

In this step, your task is to determine how you wish to reveal your Consequence to your readers. Some Consequences, like the smoldering volcano above the town, are more or less self-evident. But in a deep character study story, the Consequence may only become apparent near the end, when the Main Character is on the verge of achieving his or her Goal. This character's motivation may be the fear of this unspoken consequence, which ultimately must be specified.

The Consequence in *The Godfather*, is only stated outright in the middle of the film, when the failing Don (Marlon Brando) succinctly tells his son Michael (Al Pacino) that if Michael fails to achieve a unified family, they will all be like puppets, rather than rulers.

Even before the Consequence is specifically revealed, it can often be felt like a pall, hanging over the story, or at least over some of the characters. And the actions of characters can ultimately be more driven by fear of the Consequence than desire for the Goal.

In this step, describe how you will reveal the nature of the Consequence to your readers, then list all the other ways in which the Consequence might affect the course of your story and the decisions and actions of your characters.

~ Step 70 ~

Success or Failure?

You've already determined that your story ends in a complete or partial Success or Failure. And you've developed a standard or yardstick against which that can be measured. Now you need to tell your audience/reader how to read that measuring stick.

You'll also want to consider the moral or message implications of the outcome, the impact on your characters, and how the outcome affects your genre, such as in a bitter-sweet ending, or a "feel good" story.

In this step, describe how you will reveal to your readers what would constitute a Success or Failure, and whether it is partial or complete. Then, list all the ways that Success or Failure would impact the characters and situations of your story.

~ Step 71 ~

Revised Synopsis

Drawing on all the expository material you've developed for your plot over the last few steps, rework your existing synopsis to include as much as you can.

Exposition

Part Two: Characters

~ Step 72 ~

Protagonist

This is where you want to reveal your protagonist not by their personality, but by their function in the story. There are many ways to do this. The protagonist is the person 'leading the charge', the person who accepts the quest, or the person who has the primary responsibility to achieve the story goal.

In *Austin Powers: The Spy Who Shagged Me*, the government thaws out Austin and puts the goal to him directly, thus he is identified as the protagonist.

Titanic, is a lot more subtle, and you get plenty of hints before the protagonist is actually revealed as Jack Dawson. (Rose in the Main Character.)

Throughout the beginning of the movie, Jack is actively doing things, starting things, which indicates he has the nature to be the protagonist, but is he? We can't be sure until the story goal is identified.

Even the goal is not a simple matter in Titanic, since it at first appears that the goal is to recover the lost jewel. But that is just a plot device to get the "real" story going. And this larger story is about getting Rose to break free from her smothering life-style, symbolized by her engagement – in essence, to *save* Rose, ultimately both emotionally and physically.

We are led to understand that the story is about Rose since the heart of the story is a flashback about her personal experiences on Titanic. She is trapped in an oppressive world from which the only escape appears to be death itself.

As soon as she comes in contact with Jack, however, he immediately takes on her cause, champions her, pursues her, and 'leads the charge' to change the course of her destiny. That is his primary goal and the true goal of the story at large, and he achieves it.

In the end, we learn of the disposition of the jewel, but that is just to provide a "book-end" that wraps the present day plot around the real story of Titanic.

So, like the exposition of most story elements, revealing the protagonist may be straight-forward or progressive.

Additionally, don't forget to consider how the protagonist might interact with other story points such as Emotional relationships and situational relationships. For example, how does being a protagonist affect your marriage if your partner is the antagonist?

In this step, then, describe how you will reveal that a particular character is the protagonist, and then list all the other scenarios that come to mind in which being a protagonist impacts and is impacted by other story points.

~ Step 73 ~

Antagonist

Revealing the antagonist is a little easier than revealing the protagonist. The antagonist, in short, is the person opposed to the protagonist achieving his or her goal. For example, if the protagonist is trying to marry the princess, the antagonist is trying to stop him, and perhaps, even trying to marry her instead. Therefore, It is often a good idea to reveal the antagonist in relationship to the goal.

In this step, describe how you will reveal to your readers which of your characters is the antagonist. Then describe other scenarios in which the antagonist influences and is influenced by other story points.

~ Step 74 ~

Protagonist Personal

So far you have a character with the role of protagonist laid over it. But how does this character's personality affect the protagonist function, and vice versa? How do these two aspects combine or conflict?

The object of this step is to humanize the protagonist, to weave the function through the character's personality to make a seamless person. You want to think of specific instances, scenes, and dialogues where the audience can clearly observe how the personality of the character responds to and also moderates the role of protagonist.

And while you're at it, consider how the personality and function of the protagonist both respond to and are impacted by other characters and other story points.

In this step, describe how you will reveal to your readers the impact of your protagonist's personality on his or her function.

~ Step 75 ~

Antagonist Personal

As with the previous step, the purpose here is to explore how this character's function as an antagonist is influenced by its personality and vice versa. The object is to create a complete and seamless character in whom the audience cannot tell where the antagonist leaves off and the person begins.

This purpose can be helped by describing scenarios in which you explore the interaction of the antagonist's personality with other characters, and in regard to other story points.

In this step, describe how you will reveal to your readers the impact of your antagonist's personality on his or her function.

~ Step 76 ~

Main Character View

Even if your Main Character is also your protagonist or antagonist, he or she will still have a view of him or her self and his or her conflict with the other character over the goal.

The protagonist and antagonist are primarily identified by their functions in the plot. This can lead your readers to view these characters objectively, and not to become as emotionally involved with them.

Unless you specifically work out a means for expressing the Main Character's view to your audience, you will lose much of the first-hand involvement with the effort to achieve the goal.

In this step, describe the specific moments by which you will reveal to your readers the Main Character's overall view of your protagonist, antagonist and the conflict between them

~ Step 77 ~

Structural Roles

Previously you have chosen archetypes (structural roles) for your characters. Now you need to describe how the audience will be shown which role each character fulfills. Again, use specific examples, scenes or dialogue.

The best way to do this, of course, is to build those examples around other story points. Show how each character's role determines how they respond to and are affected by other story points you have developed. This will help integrate the actions of your characters into the overall unfolding of your story.

You task in this step is to describe how you will reveal to your readers the structural roles of each of your characters.

~ Step 78 ~

Structural Relationships

You have already worked out the structural (archetypal) relationships among your characters. But how will the audience know what these relationships are? In this step, describe the specific scenes or moments you will use to reveal these relationships to your audience.

Relationships might be established in an argument, a conversation between two characters about two or more other characters, or even in a newspaper headline or answering machine message. Be inventive! But make sure you spell out exactly how your readers will come to know the nature of these relationships.

~ Step 79 ~

Situational Relationships

As with the previous question, you should look for interesting ways of dropping expository information about your novel's situational relationships (who is married to, works for or is contractually obligated to whom).

Still, even if nothing inventive comes to mind, a straightforward reveal is better than no reveal at all! At some point, one way or another, you need to make sure your audience knows who is related to whom and in what way.

For example, a man is working at his desk in a busy office. A woman rushes in, storms up to the desk, slaps him across the face and marches back out the door. Rubbing his face, he looks up to see his co-workers staring at him and says, "My wife."

In this step, describe how you will reveal to your readers the situational relationships that exist among your characters. Use specific examples of scenes or moments.

~ Step 80 ~

Emotional Relationships

Emotional relationships begin with a "baseline" and then evolve. You will need to establish how your characters feel about one another at the beginning of your story. Later, in the Storytelling stage, you'll describe the growth of these emotional relationships over the course of the story.

Both characters in a relationship need not be present to establish how they connect. You might give your readers a look at one character's room where he keeps a score of framed pictures of the second character, his female co-worker, in a little shrine.

Then, you describe the second character's room where there is but a single picture of the first character which has been made into a dartboard. It is obviously well used as evidenced by the great quantity of dart holes. There are three darts in it as another slams in to join it, thrown by the second character.

Or, one character might write a story about the other for a newspaper or a school report. A photo album might show two people in a series of pictures over the years.

In Citizen Kane, the relationship between Kane and his wife is established by a series of vignettes over the years in which the size of their dinner table grows, moving them farther and farther away from each other.

Of course, in real life most emotional relationships are not a single melody but a rich and complex symphony. You may want to develop a different specific means of revealing each aspect of a complex emotional relationship, or you might prefer to have a single illustration that reveals the complexity all at once.

Again, even if you can't think of an inventive reveal now, at least put in a placeholder example that you can fall back on if the Muse fails you. Make sure that the audience is absolutely made aware of every important emotional relationship among your characters.

In this step, then, describe how you will reveal to your readers the emotional relationships that exist among your characters. Use specific story scenes or moments.

~ Step 81 ~

Revised Synopsis

For this step, revise your existing synopsis to incorporate as much as possible of the material you have created in this section for the exposition of your characters.

Exposition

Part Three:
Theme

~ Step 82 ~

Thematic Conflict

You have already established your message issue, such as "greed." And, you have established your counterpoint, such as "generosity." Now is the time to consider them together as in "Greed vs. Generosity."

It is one thing to tell your audience, "Greed leads to self-destruction." It is another thing to prove it! Using such a premise as the basis for your theme provides you with clear idea of what you hope to say, but it provides precious little guidance in how to say it.

You should focus on the Emotional Argument as the way to prove your point without resorting to cut-and-dried, ham-handed, generalizations and platitudes. Here's how it works:

"Greed," in our example premise, does not really stand alone, but has the counter-point of "Generosity." Although the focus of our story will be on Greed, by also showing the contrasting impact of Generosity, we create a thematic conflict pitting point against counter-point.

In your story you need to explore both point and counterpoint several times to see the relative worth of each. BUT, you should never compare both *directly*. Rather, the thematic point should be explored on several occasions to see how it fares. Interwoven in other scenes or moments, the counterpoint needs to be separately explored to see how it fares on its own.

As the story progresses, your readers will begin to tally-up the independent value of each, averaging its benefits with its drawbacks. By the end of the story, when all examples of the worth of both point and counter-point have been presented, the audience will arrive at an emotional conclusion that one is better than the other.

For example, Greed may seem to have a greatly negative impact in its first appearance, but slightly positive results in its second. A third appearance might see it as being neutral. Overall, the average of all three appearances rates it as slightly negative.

In contrast, Generosity might also appear greatly negative at first, then highly positive, then slightly positive. In the end, it averages out as slightly positive. The conclusion for the audience is that Greed is somewhat worse than Generosity.

Emotions don't see things as black and white. By avoiding the simple blanket statement made by a premise and "arguing" the relative worth of point and counter-point over the course of your story, you will create an "emotional argument" which will sway your readers to your point of view, rather than trying to hit them over the head.

In this step, describe how you reveal to your readers the growing thematic conflict in your story through a series of independent illustrations of the benefits and/or detriments of each side of the thematic argument.

~ Step 83 ~

Revised Synopsis

Here's another simple but important step: revise your synopsis to include the exposition of your thematic conflict.

Exposition

Part Four: Genre

~ Step 84 ~

Genre Atmosphere

The old saying that the whole is greater than the sum of the parts is particularly apt when considering Genre.

For example, the purpose of a Horror story is not to "hit the marks" by including all the proper elements of a Horror story, but to actually create a sense of horror in the reader.

Step back from your story from a moment. Consider the way you want your readers to feel about it when the story is over. Then, look back over your list of genre elements and begin to think of them as parts of a mosaic that will ultimately become a single emotional picture of your story.

Create groups of elements that you think fit particularly well together to create a greater impact than they do individually.

Now, write a description for each of your genre element groups in such a way that it specifies the collective impact of the group on your readers and how the elements in each group will all work together to create a greater experience.

~ Step 85 ~

Revised Synopsis

Revise your synopsis to include the exposition of your genre's atmosphere as developed in the last step.

Storytelling

Part One: Plot

~ Step 86 ~

Plot - Act One

In the Exposition Stage you created specific manners and instances in which your story elements will be revealed to your readers. Here in the Storytelling Stage, you are going to work out the order in which each of these instances will come into play.

A good way to organize your material in a sequence is to divide it in acts. Though the number of acts in a novel can vary, there are usually at least three.

Act one introduces the story problem and goal, the protagonist, antagonist and main character, the overlying thematic topic and underlying thematic message, and establishes the edges of the novel's unique genre.

Act two develops the details of all the material introduced in act one and also initiates new connections among elements of the plot and among characters. In additions, difficulties, obstacles and unexpected turns of events complicate the effort to achieve the goal, befuddle the main character's quest for a personal resolution, advance the stakes riding on the thematic issues, and enrich the atmosphere of the genre.

Act three brings all the dramatic tensions that were amplified by the difficulties of act two into conjunction in a series of conflicts leading to an overall climax at the end upon which hinges blot the logistic and passionate outcome of all that has happened.

Following act three is a concluding scenario, or a collection of moments in which the individual outcomes for each problem in the plot, the personal goals and issues of each character, a confirmation of the thematic message and the icing on the genre are all addressed, wrapped up and dismissed.

As usual, we begin each stage with plot. We'll follow plot through all three acts and the conclusion, then move on to develop the act sequences for your characters, theme and genre.

The first step in creating your plot timeline is to pull from the material you have already developed all the plot elements you'd like to appear in the first act of your novel.

In regard to plot, act one is about the *set up*. It establishes the way things are when the problem begins. It introduces the problem, establishes the goal and its requirements, as well as the consequences if the goal is not achieved.

Many stories include a journey or quest that leads to the goal. In such stories, the first act concerns discovery of the need for and nature of the quest (be it logistic or personal and passionate), the acceptance of the quest, and preparations to embark. Act one then concludes with the final preparations and a restatement of the necessity of the quest by reminding the readers of the potential consequences.

In all stories, by the end of act one, your readers must understand what the story is about, what is to be achieved, and how the effort toward that end is expected to proceed.

Keep in mind that for storytelling purposes you may intend to fool your audience into believing the goal is one thing when it will later turn out to be another.

Also, the plot of many stories includes a "teaser" at the very beginning of the act. The teaser is an emotional "hook" meant to snare generate interest and draw your readers into your book.

Almost every television episode begins with a teaser to keep the audience from changing the channel.

Teasers may or may not have anything to do with the story at large. Sometimes they are simply exciting emotional or action-oriented extravaganzas which are nothing more than entertainment, and add little to the structure of the real story about to begin.

In any event, by the end of the first act, your readers must feel they understands what the story is about and the direction it appears to be taking.

For this step, review your plot exposition material from the Exposition Stage and list the plot points (or instances of plot points) you'd rather reveal to your readers toward the beginning of your novel, rather than in the middle or at the end.

~ Step 87 ~

Plot - Act Two

This is the act of development. The second act further develops plot points that you set up in your first act, adding richness and detail to your story and adding any new plot information that will come into play near the middle of your novel.

If there's a journey in your story, act two is about the beginning and progress of that quest. As progress is made, the obstacles to progress become more substantial. Every step taken towards that goal increases in difficulty.

Somewhere in act two there is a major plot twist, due either to new information uncovered or some physical or logistic change that throws the whole story into left field.

In some stories this twist happens in the middle of the act. The second half of the act is then spent trying to recover from the set back and begin anew. In other stories, this twist occurs at the end of the second act, driving the quest in a whole new direction for the beginning of act three.

In all cases, the plot development in act two adds to the detail of each plot point and the complexity of the web that holds them all together.

In this step, review your plot exposition material and list the plot points you wish to reveal to your readers in the middle of your novel.

~ Step 88 ~

Plot - Act Three

This is the act of the climax. The whole of the third act is building up to that point, creating tension and suspense. This is what your entire novel has been leading up to. You want your third act to be more fast-paced than the rest of your story, and a lot more suspenseful.

The most compelling stories build the forces for and against the goal so that each becomes stronger and stronger. At the point of climax each is so powerful that something has to give - the tension is just too great. And yet, since they are balanced, the outcome is still uncertain.

The progression of the third act of plot is often heavily influenced by genre. For example, a compelling mystery might be designed to spread suspicion even wider than before, rather than narrowing in on just a few characters. Therefore, the sense of building tension may spring from increasing confusion, rather than understanding.

In all cases, act three must involve all loose ends of your plot and draw all dynamic forces to a head.

In this step, review your plot exposition material and list the plot points you wish reveal to your readers toward the end of your novel.

After you have completed this step there should be no unused plot exposition material remaining. If there is, rework your lists for acts one, two and three to incorporate it.

~ Step 89 ~

Plot - Act One Beginning

Now we'll get more detailed and divide each of the three acts into three parts, beginning, middle, and end.

The beginning of act one is the teaser. It may or may not have anything to do with the actual plot of the story. This is where you get the feel of the story and the feel of the main character. A good example is in Raiders of the Lost Ark. In the very beginning Indiana Jones replaces a statue with a bag of sand and then gets chased through a lot of booby traps. This actually has nothing to do with the story to come, but it sets the tone and grips the audience.

In character driven novels, the plot teaser is often an introduction to the troubles of the principal characters in order to draw the reader into, among other things, buying the book.

In atmospheric novels, the plot teaser is an opportunity to introduce the reader to the kind of events from which the plot will be comprised, thereby establishing a context that will flavor all that happens in the plot for the course of the novel.

Referring to the material you selected for the first act, describe the exposition you wish to reveal to your audience right off the bat, as your story opens.

~ Step 90 ~

Plot - Act One Middle

The middle of act one should be designed to set up the situation and goal. Even though you should reveal the goal in this section, you don't need to have the protagonist accept the goal at this time.

If your goal requires a lot of preparation before starting on the quest, then you might want to have the acceptance of the goal by the end of this section and the preparation in the next section.

In contrast, if your protagonist needs to think or to do something before accepting the goal and/or there is no preparation needed before the quest, then the acceptance of the goal can happen in the end section of the first act instead.

Referring the material you selected for the first act, describe the plot exposition you wish to reveal as your story begins to unfold.

~ Step 91 ~

Plot - Act One Ending

By the end of act one everyone and everything should be ready to embark on the quest. All preparation, all acceptance is completed. Just as when you are going on vacation you turn off all the lights, pet the pets, lock the doors, put the suitcases in the car, get in the car, put on your seatbelt, start the car and drive off out of sight... all this must be completed by the end of the first act. The second act begins with the car on the road.

Referring the material you selected for the first act, describe the remaining exposition that has not yet been revealed, which will bring your first act to a close.

Be sure all of the material you listed in act one has now been distributed into sections one, two or three.

~ Step 92 ~

Plot - Act Two Beginning

This section presents the beginning of the quest. It is the start of the actual journey. In many stories, this is an upbeat or at least hopeful time. Everything goes as planned. Keep in mind that as act two progresses the difficulties in achieving the goal are constantly increasing. This is the generally the section before that starts to happens; when it seems as if the journey will be a piece of cake or at least easily accomplished.

Referring to the material you selected for your plot for the second act, describe the exposition you wish to reveal to your audience right off the bat, kicking off or setting up the second act.

~ Step 93 ~

Plot - Act Two Middle

This is possibly the most important section you will write in your plot timeline. It is the midpoint, the exact center of your story.

Act two has in it, either in this section or the end section, a special problem, often called a "plot twist." The stakes are raised in an unexpected form, and in so-doing the whole picture is changed.

In an action story it will change what the characters think they need to do and make the goal more difficult to achieve. In a character piece, this problem makes it more difficult to resolve their personal problems; it complicates them.

Now you have a choice to make. If your plot twist will require reorganization or recovery by the characters, then it should be in this section. But if the plot twist simply sends things in a new direction, then it should be at the end of the next section.

Referring the material you selected for the second act, describe the plot exposition you wish to reveal as the act begins to unfold.

~ Step 94 ~

Plot - Act Two Ending

In the last step you have determined either to put a ground-shaking problem in the previous middle section of act two, or you are planning to put it in this one.

Remember that if your characters' mid-novel turning-point problem requires a major reorganization of their plans, then it should have been in the last section leaving this section for them to reorganize and/or recover. But if you chose to put the problem in this section, make sure the problem does not require substantial reorganization, just a change or direction beginning in act three.

You can have act two go out with a bang if you drop your plot twist right at the end of this section. Or, if the bang was in the middle section you can have this section (and act two) go out with a whimper.

Now don't let the word fool you, a *whimper* can be very effective. As an example, suppose in the middle of act two a natural disaster occurs as the Plot Twist bang. All the food the group has with them is scattered to the winds. After this disaster, all the food that can be found must be found.

The end section of act two in such a story would involve finding the food, patching bags, rounding up lost horses, fixing what's broken and so on, recovering.

At the very last, everything is ready to go, and the character who is carrying the final food sees a last grain of rice on a rock, picks it up, drops it in a bag, gets on his horse and leaves with the group.

That moment with the single grain of rice is the whimper. It ends the act with a subtle sense of closure and the anticipation that act three will begin with a new sense of purpose and new challenges for the characters.

Referring the material you selected for the second act, describe the remaining exposition that has not yet been revealed, drawing the second act to a close.

~ Step 95 ~

Plot - Act Three Beginning

Act three is the buildup to and, of course, the climax itself. All the plot points in the story have been set up in the first act, developed in the second, and the third act is where everything comes together for better or for worse.

The beginning of the third act is a response to the plot twist of the second act. If you put the twist in the middle of the second act, then the characters spent the remaining part of act two recovering from that set back and getting ready to start again. In such a case, the beginning of act three feels like the beginning of the quest all over again - with renewed resolve.

If you put the twist at the end of the second act, then it dropped like a bombshell and changed the whole purpose of what the characters are trying to achieve. In this case, act three begins with the characters setting off in a whole new direction than at the beginning of the quest.

Either way, the reader should be made to know that this is the start of the final push toward the ultimate climax or reckoning.

Referring to the material you selected for the third act, describe the exposition you wish to reveal to your audience right off the bat, kicking off the final drive toward the climax.

~ Step 96 ~

Plot - Act Three Middle

Throughout your novel, although the protagonist and antagonist may have come into conflict, there have always been extenuating circumstances that prevented an ultimate conflict. In the middle of act three, these circumstances are dismantled, one by one, until nothing more stands between these two principal characters.

At the end of this section it is clear that a final face-off is inevitable.

Referring the material you selected for the third act, describe the plot exposition you wish to reveal as the plot picks up speed toward the climax.

~ Step 97 ~

Plot - Act Three Ending

This is climax of your story. It is where the antagonist and protagonist meet for the final conflict. Your entire story has been leading up to this moment, with rising tension and suspense. All the stops are removed and the momentum cannot be turned aside.

When the protagonist and antagonist meet, they start with the small stuff, sizing each other up. This is true whether it is an action-oriented story or a character study. The dynamics are the same - only the weapons they use are different.

In action stories there will be physical weapons. In character stories, the weapons will be emotional. In stories about a single character grappling with personal problems, his or her demons come to bear, slowly but directly, building to the final breaking point.

In all kinds of stories, this section builds as the two camps (and their followers) pull stronger and stronger weapons out of their arsenal, since the smaller ones have proven ineffective.

The battle quickly becomes more heated, more imperative, and riskier. Eventually both the antagonist and protagonist have employed all the weapons they have at their disposal except one – the Big One. They each retain a trump card, one last weapon that they have not yet used for fear that it might backfire or take them down along with their opponent. With the use of this last weapon the battle will be decided, one way or another.

The final moments of the ending of act three might take one of two directions:

1. The weapon (physical or emotion) is employed and the results are seen as the smoke clears.

2. The weapon is employed and the result is left in limbo until the conclusion (epilog, dénouement or "wrap-up")

Referring the material you selected for the third act, describe the remaining exposition that has not yet been revealed, bringing your entire story to a climax.

~ Step 98 ~

Plot Conclusion

The conclusion is the aftermath and epilog. The climax is over and it's time to take stock of all that has happened.

The conclusion is both a cool down period for the reader after the excitement of the climax and is also a wrap up of loose ends.

How did it all turn out? What was gained and what was lost? Was the effort to achieve the goal successful or not. Or, what the Goal only partially achieved, and was that partial achievement enough?

In a sense, the conclusion is a new "set-up." Just as the opening of your story set-up the way things are when the problem begins, the conclusion sets up how things are, now that it is over.

What kind of new situation has come into being through the changes wrought by the climax?

In later sections we'll deal with the conclusion to the Character, Theme, and Genre elements of your story. For this question, concentrate only on how things end up in regard to the plot.

For this final step in your lot timeline, describe the state of affairs as your story wraps up.

Storytelling

Part Two: Characters

~ Step 99 ~

Character Intros – Act One

The arc of each character's development in your novel can be divided into four sections: Intros, Growth, Climax and Dismissal. This holds true not only for their roles but for the relationships among them as well.

Introductions are usually completed by the end of act one, growth is the focus of act two, rising tension toward a climax is developed in act three, and dismissals are addressed in the denouement or wrap-up, though could occur at any time if a character dies, leaves, or is replaced by another doing the same job.

In the Exposition section, you have already determined something of the manner in which you will reveal your characters' roles and relationships. Now you must figure out specifically in what order to reveal this information about your characters so they are established as real people.

You might tell your readers all there is to know about a particular character right up front. But for another character, you may drop little bits of information over the whole course of the story keeping them mysterious and adding to the intrigue. And, of course, you want to note how a character's outlook and feelings change as the story unfolds.

Then there is the question of who shows up first? Joe, Tom, Sally, or the Monster? Perhaps you wish to first introduce a supporting character and follow him or her until they latch up with a major character. Or, you might reveal several characters together in a group activity.

Who is your Main Character? Do you want to involve your audience immediately by bringing that character in first, or would you rather have them look more objectively at the characters and plot, introducing the Main Character later?

As has already been said, you know all about your characters while your audience knows nothing. It's okay to reveal more about your characters later in the story, but you must lay the groundwork and reveal personality so that your readers can sympathize with their situation and feel for them as the story progresses. For complex characters, it may take the entire story before all their subtleties are revealed.

Sometimes an author may want to have a character with a dark side, or a hidden side that will be revealed only later in the story. Don't avoid introducing such a character, but rather try to introduce its facade as a complete character, making it that much more shocking when they reveal their other face.

Remember, first impressions are lasting, and an audience with the first impression of someone as a good guy, will resist thinking of them as a bad guy for as long as possible. So, don't give hints to the truth right off the bat.

For this step, refer to the exposition material you developed for your characters and then describe how each of your characters is introduced to your readers as a person for the very first time in act one of your novel.

~ Step 100 ~

Structural Role Intros – Act One

In the previous step you determined how and when you are going to introduce your characters to your readers in act one. In this step, you are going to work out how to reveal each character's structural role (such as protagonist or the Trickster Archetype).

You have already determined in the Exposition section the manner in which the structural (or archetypal) roles of your characters are revealed. Now all you need to do is figure out how this actually unfolds relative to your characters' introduction as people in act one.

You may wish to reveal the structural role at the same time you introduce the character's personality as determined in the previous step. Or, you may reveal the structural role before introducing the personality of the character. Certainly, you don't have to follow the same pattern for every character. In fact, mixing it up a bit can add a degree of interest to this necessary process.

Again, the real question is who goes first? If you previously decided to introduce several characters' roles at once, perhaps in an argument or a professional meeting, when does this occur in relation to the introduction of their personalities in the previous step?

You may choose to have some characters already established by personality, then introduce their structural roles and the roles of others in the argument. Later, the personalities would be revealed for the characters who were first introduced by role alone in the argument.

As you can see, although we have separated the introductions of the characters, structural roles, structural relationships, situational relationships, and emotional relationships, several of them may actually occur at the same time.

In this step, then, briefly describe the manner in which you will introduce each character's structural role (such as protagonist or antagonist) relative to their introductions as personalities in act one.

~ Step 101 ~

Structural Relationship Intros – Act 1

So far in act one you have worked out the manner in which you will introduce your characters as people and how the introduction to each character's structural role might be integrated into that and in what order.

In this step, build on those introductions and the material you have already developed in the Exposition Stage regarding your characters' structural relationships.

Weave as many of these structural relationship introductions as you can into the moments you already devised in the last two steps. In this way, you won't get stuck individually introducing just the characters' identities, then all their structural roles, then structural relationships and so on, which would be stilted and predictable.

In short, briefly describe how you will introduce the structural relationships among your characters to your readers in act one of your novel.

~ Step 102 ~

Situational Relationship Intros – Act One

Situational relationships (such as being married, being siblings, business partners or in a chain of command) come in major and minor varieties. Characters may be involved in any number of these relationships with any number of other characters.

Some authors prefer to get the most important relationships out of the way first, and then refine the reader/audience understanding with less compelling relationships later. Other authors like to start with the subtle situational relationships, then put them in context with the more broad stroke relationships.

The order in which relationships are revealed doesn't change the substance of the story, but significantly alters the experience of the story for your readers.

You have already developed ideas for how to reveal each situational relationship independently in the Exposition Stage, but in this step, briefly describe how you will introduce the situational relationships among your characters relative to one another.

In other words, you might reveal several relationships in an argument and several others independently both before and after that argument.

So for this step, work out if and how you will group these introductions and in what order.

~ Step 103 ~

Emotional Relationship Intros – Act One

Emotional relationships are like pungent spices. Too little, and the dish is bland, too much, and it is too hot to palate. The progression of your story needs to be peppered with the might amount at the right place.

Too few scenes developing the emotional relationships and the story will be dry and fail to inspire your audience with sympathy for your characters. Too many and your story will be sappy and will inspire nausea instead.

In the Exposition Stage you've already determined the manner in which each emotional relationship will be revealed. In this step describe order or sequence in which they will unfold.

~ Step 104 ~

Structural Relationship Growth – Act Two

Structural relationships are based on the natures of your

characters as archetypes such as protagonist, antagonist, Tempter, Wise Woman, Fool, etc.

Earlier, you described the nature of the structural relationships you wish to explore among your characters and how you will reveal them to your audience in act one. Now you must determine how you want those relationships to change as the story unfolds in act two.

Since archetypes must maintain their structural roles if the dramatic structure is to be sound, any growth in structural relationships must come from the degree of intensity of the relationship under a progression of experiences and situations.

For example, suppose a protagonist has a structural relationship with a Wise Woman archetype. The protagonist will always drive the plot forward when no one else has the motivation. But how strongly will he or she be driven? What if a major obstacle has all but obliterated the team and the future looks bleak. Certainly the protagonist is not likely to jump up with pompoms and cheer on the troops! Rather, he or she would express the need to continue, and the reasons why, but perhaps in a subdued manner.

The Wise Woman might have a brilliant insight to offer that clinches the argument made by the protagonist. Or, she might have deep thoughts that would argue against the protagonist. Or, she might even have some almost stupid comment like, "It is darkest before the dawn." In that case, the protagonist might comment with somber humor that this advice wasn't up to the Wise Woman's usual standards. She might then say, "Well, they can't all be gems..."

In this example, both protagonist and Wise Woman maintain their structural natures, but how the relationship grows between them has many possibilities. Just because the protagonist is always for the goal doesn't mean anyone else has to be. And the level of intensity of each character's archetypal function can fluctuate with the events over the course of the story.

So, what you need to do here is refer to the relationships you have already planned, consider the progression of your plot, and then describe the growth of each structural relationship from its initial state as established in act one through the tribulations of act two.

~ Step 105 ~

Situational Relationship Growth – Act Two

Each character may have a number of different situational relationships with other characters, and may even have several relationships with single characters. For example, Jane may be Tom's wife, but also his boss at the bank. Furthermore, situational relationships can change all the time. As when Tom gets promoted and is now Jane's boss!

So if you have a cop and a subordinate, what happens if one transfers to a different unit? What if two brothers find out that one was adopted? How does a construction worker deal with the discovery that he is really a secret agent with amnesia, and his wife is his control agent, as in "Total Recall?"

Previously, you have determined what you want your characters' situational relationships to be, and how you intend to reveal them. But that is just a starting point. Now you should let yourself go! Consider your plot, incorporate unexpected changes in situational relationships, and list them here for every relationship for every set of characters you wish to explore.

If you usually have your characters maintain their situational relationship throughout the story, you can break free of that plodding predictability and add surprise and life here.

For this step, describe how your characters grow in their situational relationships in act two. Be sure all situational relationships are addressed, even if you choose to maintain them without growth.

~ Step 106 ~

Emotional Relationship Growth – Act Two

Perhaps the most complex relationships among characters are the emotional ones because they can grow to any degree in any direction AND because both characters don't have to feel the same way about each other!

For example, how many stories are written about "unrequited love" where one character is infatuated with the other, but the other is repulsed by them. Another example is the younger brother who tags along with the older brother. To the younger, the older brother is his hero. To the older, the younger brother is a pest.

Now, suppose the younger brother is attacked by a bully. The older brother may come to the rescue and defend his tag-along. But the moment the threat is gone and the younger brother looks up at his protector with glowing eyes, the older brother say, "Okay, get out of here and leave me alone." Emotional relationships change with the slightest breeze and change back with the least provocation.

Consider the emotional relationships you have already determined you wish to explore, and the manner in which you devised to reveal them to your reader/audience in the Exposition Stage. Now, consider your plot and changes in situational relationships. Consider the emotional journey of your characters as individuals. Then, describe how each emotional relationship might shift, change, and grow for each of the characters in each emotional relationship.

It is a fair amount of work, but you will find that this development more than any other will enrich your characters and the passionate experience of your story.

This step's task: describe how your characters grow in their Emotional relationships in act two.

~ Step 107 ~

Structural Relationship Climax – Act Three

For act two, you have developed the nature and growing intensity of the structural relationships among your characters (their relationships based on dramatic function, such as protagonist or the Reason Archetype. Now in act three, you will turn up the volume.

Each relationship should come under additional strain so that tension in the structural relationship rises. To accomplish this, you need to create dramatic moments in which outside pressures put each character's structural role and hence the relationships among them in an increasing vice-grip.

For light comedies, romance stories, and so on, structural relationship issues are often not all that crucial. In fact, overemphasizing tension based on structural relationships alone might be detrimental in particular genres. So keep an eye toward the emphasis you want for the dramatic structure of your novel, and within that scope, bring tension to its maximum by the end of the third act.

Tension does not have to rise smoothly, but can lurch forward in fits and starts. Tension can rise slowly, then drop quickly in a momentary release, only to begin to rise again. Or, it can snap into place precipitously, only to gradually fade away. In fact, a single relationship might employ both of these techniques! The key is to mimic real life and the uneven nature of the stress in our lives, idealized in stories.

Ultimately, you will want to arrive at a set of dramatic circumstances that brings each structural relationship to the maximum stress level appropriate to your genre. That is the point at which the relationship will stand or snap - the character climax of your novel.

In terms specifically of structural relationships, you have already established the kinds of situations and considerations that put each relationship under strain in the material you developed for act two. Now is the time to build on that material.

In psychology, there are two kinds of stimulus that bring one to a point of tension:

1. Spatial Summation - in which a single, very tense situation makes a large impact all at once.

2. Temporal Summation - in which a series of small situations build upon one another until the strain is at a maximum.

Either approach works equally well when building tension in character relationships.

Now, for this step, develop and describe the rising tension and climax of each structural relationship based on your characters' dramatic functions such as antagonist or Tempter.

~ Step 108 ~

Situational Relationship Climax – Act Three

Unlike structural relationships, the nature of situational relationships can change or threaten to change over the course of the story. In act two, you have already outlined the kinds of changes that are being threatened. Now, in act three, it is time to revisit these threatened or actual changes and put the relationships to the test.

For example, if in act two Jane was Tom's boss, and he was up for a promotion, in act three he gets it, making Tom Jane's boss. But, if in act two Tom had already been promoted over Jane, he gets demoted again, back into her department.

To reach maximum tension, the situational relationship does not actually have to change, but it must at least reach the maximum potential to change. Whether it does or not is the actual moment of climax.

Keep in mind that not all relationships require stress and climax. But at least some of them need to evolve in that manner to involve your reader/audience.

For this step, develop and describe the rising tension and climax of each situational relationship as it occurs in act three.

~ Step 109 ~

Emotional Relationship Climax – Act Three

The emotional relationships among your characters are the most complex of your story. To understand each relationship fully, and to ensure that each doesn't skip a beat, it is best to follow them through one by one. But when it comes to actually weaving them all into your story, you may find dramatic moments that bring a number of your characters together in such a way that several of these relationships come into play at the same time.

For example, though you may have established an emotional relationship between a father and son and another between the son and his girlfriend, when they all end up in the same elevator, both relationships come into play with the son at the fulcrum. In fact, a new emotional relationship may be established between the father and girlfriend where none had existed before since they had never met.

You have built your characters' relationships from the very start of your novel. But in life, new relationships come into being all the time. Similarly, as you develop your story it takes on a life of its own. It is only natural if new relationships come into being along the way. In fact, it would probably be unnatural if they didn't.

Yet whenever they are created, all emotional relationships must eventually reach a climax in your story by the end of act three.

For this step, look back over the introduction and growth of your characters' relationships that you have already established. Based on how they are converging, develop and describe the rising tension and climax of each emotional relationship in act three.

~ Step 110 ~

Dismissals

Over the course of the story, your readers have come to know your characters and to feel for them; they are emotionally invested in them. Every attribute, every relationship – structural, situational and emotional, needs to be dismissed to satisfy your readers and illustrate the final disposition of those they have come to care about.

In addition, the reader needs a little time to say goodbye - to let the each character walk off into the sunset or to mourn for them before the novel ends.

This is the conclusion, the wrap-up or denouement. After everything has happened to your characters, after the final showdowns with their respective demons, what are they like? How have they changed?

If a character began the story as a skeptic, does it now have faith? If they began the story full of hatred for a mother that abandoned them, have they now discovered revelations to the effect that she was forced to do this, and now they no longer hate?

These are the kinds of things you need to tell your readers: how your characters' journeys changed them, whether they resolved their problems, and so on.

And in the end, it is character dismissals that constitute a large part of your story's message. It is not enough to know if a story ends in success or failure, but also if the characters are better off emotionally or plagued with even greater demons, regardless of whether or not the goal was achieved.

You can show what happens to your characters directly or through a conversation by others about them or even in a post-script on each after the story is over as a series of fictional newspaper clippings.

How you do this is limited only by your creative inventiveness, but make sure you review each character and each relationship and provide at least a minimal dismissal for each.

For this step, develop and describe the ultimate disposition of each character and every relationship.

~ Step 111 ~

Characters - Act One Beginning

Now that you have dealt with the introduction, growth, climax and dismissal of your characters and their relationships, we need to get a bit more precise about the order in which all these dramatic elements will happen, beginning with the first part of act one.

Some stories introduce characters as people and then let the reader discover their roles and relationships afterward. This tends to help an audience identify with the characters.

Other stories put roles first, so that we know about the person by their function and/or job, then get closer to them as the act progresses. This tends to make the readers initially pigeonhole the characters by stereotype, and then draws them into learning more about the actual people behind the masks.

Finally, there are stories that introduce character relationships – be they situational, structural, or emotional - at the beginning. This causes the audience to see the problems among the characters but not take sides so strongly until they can learn about the people on each side of the relationship, and the roles that constrain them.

Of course, you do not have to treat these introductions equally for all characters and relationships. For example, you might introduce on character as a person, then introduce their relationship with another character, then divulge the constraints the other character is under due to role, then revel the other character as a person.

This approach would initially cast sympathy (or derision) at the first character, temper it by showing a relationship with which he or she must contend, then temper that relationship by showing the constraints of the other character, and finally humanize that other character so a true objective balance can be formed by the reader.

Don't forget that first impressions stick in our minds, and it is much easier to judge someone initially than to change that judgment later. Use this trait of audiences to quickly identify important characters up front, or to put their complete situations later, thereby forcing your readers to reconsider their attitudes, and thereby learn and grow.

No matter what approach you take, you have the opportunity to weave a complex experience for your readers, blending factual, logistic information about your characters with the readers' emotional experience in discovering this information.

For this step, then, refer to the introductions you established in act one and select the ones you want to reveal in the first part of act one, enriching them as you can from the approaches described above.

~ Step 112 ~

Characters - Act One Middle

It takes a while to fully introduce a cast of characters in all the ways we've explored. So, there are some characters, roles and relationships that will come forth in the middle and end of the first act.

Readers don't want or need to know everything about your characters right up front. They want to learn about them - to get to know them and their situations.

Sometimes this process involves discovering more about the characters, and other times it involves changing one's opinion or impression of a character, based on additional information.

So, you may wish to enhance the introductions your have just developed for the beginning of act one. For example, if you have introduced a character as your protagonist, you may wish to deepen the audience understanding of just how driven this character is to achieve the goal.

To do this, you could write an additional scenario that stands by itself, or you could create second pass at introducing the protagonist and use it as a launching pad to introduce the antagonist.

So, in this hypothetical, when the protagonist reasserts his or her motivation, the antagonist might be seen in action for the very first time by jumping in to contradict the protagonist. And this, in turn, might serve as introduction of the structural relationship between the two, and any number of other character attributes.

In this step, then, refer to both your introductions for act one and the selections you made for the beginning of act one and pull together the characters, roles, and relationships you wish to divulge next, in the middle of the first act.

~ Step 113 ~

Characters - Act One Ending

It takes a while to fully introduce a cast of characters in all the ways we've explored. So, there are some characters, roles and relationships that will come forth near the end of the first act.

The last part of the first act generally completes the introduction of your cast of major characters. Now, this is not *always* true. In some genres, such as mysteries, characters might be introduced throughout the story. But even then, there is usually some hint that such a character exists, by virtue of his influence behind the scenes. Still and all, you'll likely have a few characters you haven't yet addressed and want to introduce by the end of the first act.

Once a character has been introduced, readers want to know more about them. It is not enough to simply introduce characters, roles, and relationships, but you also need to revisit them and add a few more details to what you have already divulged.

This mimics the way we learn about people in real life: a first impression followed by a series of refinements that impression.

To address this, review the introductions you made in the beginning and middle of the first act, and consider how they might be enhanced in the process of making any new introductions you have not yet included.

For this step, describe the introductions of characters, roles, and relationships you wish to occur in the last third of the first act, and describe additional details about your previously introduced characters, seasoned to taste.

~ Step 114 ~

Characters - Act Two Beginning

Act two is all about character growth. Previously, you described how you wanted your characters to grow in their roles and relationships in the second act in general. Now, we need to get a bit more precise about the order in which specific moments of growth will occur.

The beginning of act two is an important one for your characters. While they developed impressions of one another in the first act (and your readers developed first impressions of them as well), they know little beyond the surface each presents.

In act two, some characters will grow by showing just how deep or shallow these initial attributes really are. Some will grow by revealing (intentionally or unintentionally) that they aren't necessarily exactly like the impression they had given. And others will illustrate in powerful ways just how different they really are.

Toward the end of act one, you may have divulged additional information about characters you had already introduced in the beginning and middle of that act. But this information would have been no more that further details about what you had already established for those characters.

Here at the beginning of act two, you'll be doing something different - you'll establish the direction of growth for these characters, either deeper into their existing traits or in gradual or sudden new directions. Your readers might see the first cracks in a facade, and through them, the glimmer of a more intense, more basic nature.

Beyond the roles and relationships, don't forget that your characters are people too. Though when it comes to the drama, they may be single-minded, when it comes to life in general, they should be as well-developed and diversified as any real person.

So use act two to reveal personality quirks, histories, physical maladies, and other attributes that have no direct bearing on the course of the story, but every importance to the mood and timbre of the experience for your readers.

For this step, then, refer way back to your characters' attributes and also to the introductions of them and their relationships. Then list or describe in short scenarios the additional material you'd like to reveal to your readers in the beginning of act two, beyond that which you already included in act one.

~ Step 115 ~

Characters - Act Two Middle

Growth doesn't happen overnight. It is an ongoing progression. The second act establishes an initial nature of growth in the beginning, then sets a second point in the middle. Your readers will use those two points to draw a line and get a sense of the direction of growth.

You have an interesting choice in the middle of act two. Do you want to tell your reader/audience the truth about your characters, or do you want to mislead them?

Now, it's a golden rule that you absolutely NEVER want to lie to your audience. Your readers give you their absolute trust, and if you violate it, they will pull away from your story completely. But, that doesn't mean you can't fib to them once in a while. The key is to not let them in on the trick too soon!

You've all read stories where a character we initially thought was a good guy says something so that we absolutely know he's really up to no good. What a cop-out! From that point forward, any surprise is gone, and all we have left is waiting for the moment the other characters figure it out (though they must be pretty stupid not to have seen it already).

If an author can't keep the secret, he or she shouldn't try in the first place. Better to just let the bad guys be bad guys, right from the get-go.

Keeping secrets has its own set of problems. Essentially, you have to have a reasonable explanation for everything that happens, *then* create a second set of *actual* reasons for why they happened, once you reveal a character was motivated differently than we thought.

Of course, there's a middle ground between having a character be straight-forward, or turning around 180 degrees. Usually people grow linearly, or a long a curve. Or, they stay on course, but outside pressure builds until they snap for better or worse.

So here in the middle of act two, consider that while you need to have your characters grow in some manner to prevent them from stagnating, there are a variety of ways that different characters might grow.

For this step, refer to the material you developed for character growth in act two, plus what you've already assigned to the beginning of act two. Then describe for each of your characters how you'll create a sense of direction to the growth of your characters, their roles, and relationships in the middle of act two.

~ Step 116 ~

Characters - Act Two Ending

By the end of act two you will need to have established all the tensions, bonds, and potentials among your characters that will come to be stretched to their limits during act three.

The end of act two should be an uneasy calm before the storm. It is the time at which everything falls into an uneven truce or dynamic stasis.

By this time, the characters pretty much know where they stand with one another - who's a friend, who's a foe, and who is neutral.

Keep in mind that your readers may see things differently. While a character may see another as trying to hinder him, that other character might actually be trying to protect him. At an even deeper level, the character tying to protect him might be misguided and really is hindering him! From a Zen perspective, first there is a mountain, then there is no mountain, then there is.

Use the ending of act two, then, not just to create potential among your characters in preparation for act three, but also to create potential between how characters see one another and how your readers see them.

(And if you want to go even deeper, you can mislead your readers so that later in act three, they must re-evaluate characters, roles, and relationships, based on new information that you have revealed.)

Finally, you may wish to use the conclusion of act two to create a split between characters who part ways, neither expecting nor wishing to see each other again (only to bring them together once more by circumstance or necessity at the beginning of act three.)

In the movie, *Reign of Fire*, for example, the leader of a band of marines and the leader of a group of refugees, have a fistfight at the end of the second act, and part ways as enemies.

But at the beginning of the third act, the marine has come to realize he was wrong, and the refugee leader has come to understand the marine actually had noble motivations. They establish a tense working relationship, and by the end of the story have come to respect each other.

In this step, describe how character roles and relationships lock into a final dynamic before the stress of the third act.

~ Step 117 ~

Characters - Act Three Beginning

Act three brings all your characters, their roles, and relationships to a climax. Previously, you described how your characters arrive at that climax. Now, we need to get a bit more precise about exactly how you will unfold these crucial moments - the order in which they will happen within the third act.

One might think that a climax is just the moment at which something is ultimately resolved. But in stories, it's more like a cascade.

By the end of act two, you have locked your characters into structural, situational, and emotional relationships that have set in place, like raisins in rice pudding. Being an act of growth, things jockeyed around a bit, while the pudding thickened, until they finally appear to be fixed in a strained position.

But, there is more than meets the eye. These relationships are not set, but merely stuck. Each is like a wound-up spring held by a latch, the tension building along fault-lines before an earthquake, or the floor filled with mousetraps in the movie "Mouse Hunt."

All it takes is one little trigger that springs just one of the relationships, and a domino-like cascade begins until all the relationships are sprung.

Think of it as a chain reaction. Something upsets one uneasy truce, and the resultant energy snaps two more into upheaval. They affect four more, then sixteen, and before you know it, the whole lot of them is thrashing about, almost chaotically.

What's more, just because one relationship snaps, doesn't mean it is done changing. In fact, the other snapping relationships around it tend to wind its spring all over again. So that by the end of the third act, every relationship has sprung into a new form, then built up a whole new kind of tension and is ready to spring again.

That is when final climax where it all goes up at once, like a fireworks show, and the character relationship tension is finally spent.

What triggers the first spring to snap? The plot. There will be some event, often apparently innocuous, that upsets one of the stable but tense relationships, and ultimately triggers the whole cascade.

Now keep in mind that everyone doesn't have to shift 180 degrees. Nor, do your characters have to be at high-intensity all the time. Rather, explore the moments of the springs tightening and loosening as other relationships alter under the strain.

The main things to remember are that the overall tension among characters should build over the course of the third act, and that the beginning of the third act should show how locked up potentials established by the end of act two now begin to rattle and unwind.

In this step, then, develop and describe the specific instances in which roles and relationships begin to vibrate and rearrange themselves, adding to the overall tension of your novel in the beginning of act three.

~ Step 118 ~

Characters - Act Three Middle

The middle of act three is often a breathing space for your characters: the calm before the storm. After all the tensions they have endured in the reordering of their relationships at the beginning of act three, they are willing to let the dust settle a bit and rethink their strategies before charging into the inevitable pyrotechnics of the final climax.

In baseball, they call this the "seventh inning stretch." In stories, it is called the middle of act three.

Up to this point, your characters and your readers have been on a roller coaster that's been going higher and higher in fits and starts. In the last part of the third act, the tension will rise up that final highest climb, and then plunge all the way to the bottom as the outcome of the story is determined.

As with a roller coaster, there is more of a thrill if you see that hill coming. So the middle of act three serves two purposes: First, to give your readers a little breathing room, and second, to set them up for the emotional upheaval to come.

If two characters had argued or fought at the beginning of the act, a third character might tell them they can settle their differences later, but if they keep fighting now, everyone will lose the bigger fight. Realizing the truth of this, the two characters would calm down, let the adrenaline clear out of their systems, and then focus on the job at hand with the other party as reluctant allies.

In Volleyball, there is the set-up and the spike. The end of act three is the spike, but the middle is the set-up. No matter how much of a slam-bang finish you have planned for your story, it will mean nothing without the right set-up.

So, consider what you have coming, consider where you've been, then use the middle of act three to refocus your characters on the overall goal, rather than on each other.

In this step, develop and describe specific instances in which characters are forced by circumstance to put their differences temporarily aside as they address the larger issues of the overall story.

~ Step 119 ~

Characters - Act Three Ending

The end of act three is like no other part of your story. It is where all the pieces that have been carefully established come into play and fall into place.

In action stories, there may not be much room for character climax material. In such stories, often the only character issue addressed is which side of the moral argument the Main Character will choose.

In character stories, however, it is a time for pulling out all the stops. Previously, your characters will have held something back, no matter how strongly they may feel, no matter what pressures they must bear. Since the situation up to this point was not a final reckoning, there was no need to put all their chips on the table.

But here, they recognize there is no tomorrow. It is all, or nothing, so each character will let loose, holding nothing back.

This is the time in which all the wound up tension in the spring that drives every role and relationship will let loose, one after another as the last third of act three builds in a crescendo to an ultimate moment of truth.

In this step, develop and describe the scenarios in which each of your characters, their roles, and relationships unravels and hits its maximum energy in a final conflict.

Storytelling

Part Three:
Theme

~ Step 120 ~

Establishing The Thematic Topic – Act One

The thematic topic is the subject matter of your story, such as "death," or "man's inhumanity to man." No matter what topic you will be exploring, it will contain large issues, small issues, and everything in between.

In act one, you need to introduce and establish your theme so that your audience gets a sense of the kinds of issues you'll be exploring. There are three different approaches you might take.

1. You could outline the scope of your subject matter with one or more large, definitive dramatic moments. Then, in acts two and three, you would gradually fill in smaller and smaller details, adding nuance and shading to the overall topic as the story progresses. This system is best when trying to apply topics that are often seen objectively or impersonally to everyday life.

2. Conversely, you could begin with the details in act one, then move to larger concerns as the story progresses. This is a good way to elevate topics dealing with commonplace, mundane, or work-a-day issues to philosophical or global importance.

3. Finally, you could mix it up, presenting a blend of issues ranging from the large to the small in every act. This creates a feeling that the topic is an area to explore, rather than a statement to be understood.

No matter which method you use, it needs to be set up in act one. So, look over the examples you've already developed to illustrate your thematic topic, determine which of the three approaches you wish to take, and then list the specific illustrations that you'd like to present in act one to establish that approach.

~ Step 121 ~

Establishing The Message Issue – Act One

The Message Issue and Counterpoint define the thematic argument of your story. They play both sides of the moral dilemma. The most important key to a successful thematic argument is to never, ever play the message issue and counterpoint together at the same time.

Why? Because the thematic argument is an emotional one, not one of reason. You are trying to sway your readers to adopt your moral view as an author. This will not happen if you keep showing one side of the argument as "good" and the other side as "bad" in direct comparison. Such a thematic argument would seem one-sided, and treat the issues as being black-and-white, rather than gray-scale.

In real life, moral decisions are seldom cut-and-dried. Although we may hold views that are clearly defined, in practice it all comes down to the context of the specific situation. For example, it is wrong to steal in general. But, it might be proper to steal from the enemy during a war, or from a large market when your baby is starving. In the end, all moral views become a little blurry around the edges when push comes to shove.

Statements of absolutes do not a thematic argument make. Rather, your most powerful message will deal with the lesser of two evils, the greater of two goods, or the degree of goodness or badness of each side of the argument. In fact, there are often situations where both sides of the moral argument are equally good, equally bad, or that both sides are neither good nor bad in the particular situation being explored in the story.

The way to create this more powerful, more believable, and more persuasive thematic argument is as follows:

1. Determine in advance whether each side is good, bad, or neutral.

Do this by assigning an arbitrary "value" to both the Message Issue and the Counterpoint. For example, we might choose a scale with +5 being absolutely good, -5 being absolutely bad, and zero being neutral.

If our thematic argument is Greed vs. Generosity, then Greed (our Message Issue) might be a -3, and Generosity (our Counterpoint) might be a -2. This would mean that Greed and Generosity are both bad (being in the negative) but that Generosity is a little less bad than Greed since Generosity is only a -2 and Greed is a -3.

2. Show the good and bad aspects of both the Message Issue and the Counterpoint.

Make sure the examples of each side of the thematic argument that you have already developed don't portray either side as being all good or all bad. In fact, even if one side of the argument turns out to be bad in the end, it might be shown as good initially. But over the course of the story, that first impression is changed by seeing that side in other contexts.

3. Have the good and bad aspects "average out" to the thematic conclusion you want.

By putting each side of the thematic argument on a roller coaster of good and bad aspects, it blurs the issues, just as in real life. But your readers will "average out" all of their exposures to each side of the argument and draw their own conclusions at the end of the story.

In this way, the argument will move out of the realm of intellectual consideration and become a viewpoint arrived at by feel. And, since you have not only shown both sides, but also the good and the bad of each side, your message will be easier to swallow. And finally, since you never directly compared the two sides, your readers will not feel that your message has been shoved down their throats.

So, make these determinations for your novel's theme and then in this step, describe the instances of just the Message Issue that you want to put forth as the first impression for your readers in act one.

~ Step 122 ~

Establishing Counterpoint – Act One

In this step, you not only need to determine whether the Counterpoint is good or bad, but if it is better, worse, or the same as the Message Issue, morally speaking within the specific context of your novel.

Keep in mind that the strongest thematic argument is made when the two sides of the issue are shown as independently having both good and bad attributes, and compared to one another it is not a black and white case of one being all good and the other all bad.

In the last step, you have already chosen which of the illustrations of your message issue you wish to serve as an introduction to your readers in act one.

In this step, list the examples of the Counterpoint you have already developed in the Exposition Stage that you would like to serve as your readers' first impression of the other side of your thematic argument in act one.

~ Step 123 ~

Establishing Main Character Dilemma – Act One

The Main Character's Dilemma is another tool for illustrating the thematic argument. Because your readers identify with the Main Character, when he or she wavers between the relative values of the message issue and the counterpoint, the thematic argument becomes personal. This helps make your message an emotional one for the reader, rather than an intellectual debate.

From the illustrations of your Main Character's dilemma you have already developed in the Exposition Stage, select those that will best ease the reader into that personal view of the issues as experienced by your Main Character in act one.

Describe how your readers will be introduced over the course of the first act to your Main Character's Dilemma, which is the heart of the thematic conflict in your story.

Then, devise any additional illustrations that you feel will solidly establish the central importance of that dilemma to your Main Character in act one.

~ Step 124 ~

Extending Topic – Act Two

In act one, you chose one of three methods for developing the thematic topic in your novel: large to small, small to large, and all mixed up.

If you went with the big to small, you should choose some middle-sized illustrations to occur now, providing a little more detail, but still with a fairly large perspective. Conceptually, you want to draw your readers away from an objective, global view of the topic slowly toward a more specific, individual, and focused appreciation.

If you decided to develop your topic from small to large, you will also want to be introducing middle sized examples, though the feeling you create in your readers will be different. With this approach, your readers gain a larger perspective on the smaller topic already described in detail.

If you chose to mix large, small, and medium illustrations of your topic throughout your novel, act two will continue that approach. Remember that act two is where you re-affirm the importance of your topic or conversely, alter the importance or context of what was established in act one.

Whichever method you chose, in this step the task is to select and/or develop additional illustrations of your thematic topic – moments, scenes or sequences that will provide additional depth and understanding of your topic and how it applies to your novel.

~ Step 125 ~

Extending Message Issue – Act Two

For this step, remember that the message issue and the counterpoint should each be in every act, but never in the same scene (dramatic moment) or at the same time.

Here in act two, you have the opportunity to change your readers' assessment of the value of the message issue. Through additional illustrations, an issue that originally appeared positive may be made to appear highly negative, neutral, or even more positive.

Your readers will "average out" their intuitive determination of the value of the message issue based on the mean average of its individual values in each act. Later, in act three, you will put the final spin on the message issue to create a final value judgment of that side of the emotional argument.

For now, keep in mind where you are headed so as not to tip the scale so far in act two that you might not be able to bring the final assessment to the level you want to establish by the end of act three.

From the illustrations and scenarios you have already developed in the Exposition Stage, select for act two the instances that will contribute to your message issue and give it additional depth and meaning.

~ Step 126 ~

Extending Counterpoint – Act Two

As with the message issue, your readers' assessment of the counterpoint's value is determined by repeated exposure. In act two, you might choose to simply re-affirm the value the counterpoint had in act one. Or, you could contrast that value or double up to raise it to the next level.

Consider what you have already done on the message issue side of the equation. You are not only concerned with the counterpoint by itself, but what its ultimate relative value is when compared to the message issue.

Although showing both the good and bad aspects of each side of the emotional argument helps create a subtle statement, you need to be careful not to become so subtle that you say nothing at all.

So make each illustration of your counterpoint clearly, and let the subtlety come from contrasting exposures, rather than a series of unclear examples.

From the illustrations and scenarios you have already developed in the Exposition Stage, select for act two the instances that will contribute to your thematic counterpoint and give it additional depth and meaning.

~ Step 127 ~

Extending Main Character Dilemma – Act Two

In act two the Main Character may often become more frenzied or unsettled in regard to his or her personal moral dilemma. Situations will arise where it is impossible for the Main Character to avoid confronting this dilemma. He or she may also grapple with a degree of personal anguish or frustration over the conflicting value standards in play.

Select from the examples of the Main Character Dilemma you have already created in the Exposition Stage (and/or create some new ones) that will illustrate how pressure grows on your main character that makes it more uncomfortable to avoid choosing a side and more difficult to continue to satisfy both.

~ Step 128 ~

Projecting Topic – Act Three

If you have been building your topic from grand illustrations in act one to smaller, more personal ones in act three, you are all set. That pattern will likely involve the reader personally with little additional effort.

But if you chose to build from the everyday to the philosophical, or if you chose to mix the global and individual examples of your topic throughout your story, then you run the risk of making the point but losing the passion. In this case, you may need to develop additional material to draw the reader back into your topic, while remaining true to the pattern you were building.

Aside from any inherent interest your readers may share in your chosen thematic subject matter, it will not become important to them personally unless you can relate that topic to their everyday lives.

For some topics, this happens all by itself, since the material explored is intrinsically commonplace and personal. But for more esoteric or unusual topics, you'll need to find a bridge to the ordinary.

An effective way to construct this bridge is by creating a sub-theme that reflects the grand, but impersonal, topic in microcosm. In contrast to the main theme, the sub theme will use illustrations that affect individual characters.

Looking over the examples of your topic that you have already created but not yet employed in acts one and two, select those that best reflect the impact of your topic on everyday life. Then, if you feel you topic is still not personal enough to truly involve the reader, fashion one or more sub themes by specifically developing a series of illustrations of your topic the pertain specifically to the individuals in your story.

~ Step 129 ~

Projecting Message Issue – Act Three

An old performer's adage proclaims, "Always leave 'em laughing." When it comes to theme, this truism could be paraphrased as "Always leave 'em feeling." Theme is an emotional argument, and the best way to make such an argument is by involving the reader at a personal level.

Since the message issue is the human quality that your story is about, there is already a built-in level of attachment to your readers. But people don't like to look at themselves critically. The trick, then, is to find a way to involve their emotions without pointing a finger at them.

You can draw your readers into an emotional bond with your message issue by devising illustrations that show the impact of that issue on characters they have come to care about.

Previously, the examples you incorporated into your story may have been more philosophical or conceptual. Or, they may have pertained to functional characters with which your readers have developed little empathy. But by selecting or creating examples that affect a character your readers feel for, you can indirectly ignite passions without alienating them.

Referring to the material you have already developed, select those illustrations that best describe how your message issue will show its importance to the life of the reader. If necessary, create new examples to bring the message issue home.

~ Step 130 ~

Projecting Counterpoint – Act Three

The emotional argument of your theme is between the message issue and the counterpoint. But the question arises, "How does the audience know which is the message issue and which is the counterpoint?"

Simply put, the message issue is the human quality being directly explored in your story. The counterpoint provides contrast to the message issue. In a practical sense, the message issue must appear forefront, and the counterpoint paints the background. This is accomplished solely through your storytelling approach.

The message issue is identified by being shown in sharp, definitive illustrations. The counterpoint becomes the background contrast by employing illustrations that are more generalized or nebulous.

For example, in "A Christmas Carol," Scrooge's lack of generosity is shown in defined moments of specific choices, dialogs, and actions. But the counterpoint of generosity is illustrated nebulously through the prevailing good cheer and group activities of the other characters and the populace of London in general - the giving Christmas Spirit, as it were.

In act three, if you have not done so already, you need to clearly establish which of the two sides of your thematic argument is the message issue and which is the counterpoint, using the methods described above.

For this step, choose the illustrations of your counterpoint you have already developed but not previously used in acts one and two that will show its direct importance to the life of the readers. If you don't have enough instances, develop some additional ones.

~ Step 131 ~

Projecting Main Character Dilemma – Act Three

As previously described, a character does not have to change in order to grow. Sometimes, a character can grow in his or her resolve, such as Doctor Richard Kimble in the movie, "The Fugitive," who continues to help others even at his own peril, rather than changing to become self-serving in order to escape. In fact, it is this quality of character that convinces the inflexible marshal on his trail that Kimble may in fact be innocent.

Whether or not your Main Character ultimately changes or remains steadfast in his nature, word view, or attitude toward a particular topic, he or she will be faced with a moment of truth where he or she must choose to stick with the old or adopt the new. The "old" is the Message Issue. The "new" is the Counterpoint.

In acts one and two, your Main Character grappled with a personal dilemma caused by the theme's emotional argument. In act three, this dilemma must work like a vice-grip to increase the moral tension to the point that the Main Character has no option but to choose one side or the other.

Keep in mind that just because the Message Issue is the focus, it is not necessarily the "proper" moral choice to choose it over the

Counterpoint. Unlike Dr. Kimble, Scrooge must, in fact, adopt the Counterpoint (generosity) over the Message Issue if he is to make the proper moral choice.

When building the pressure of the Main Character's Dilemma, it is often useful to employ plot events that box the Main Character into situations where he or she has fewer and fewer options by which they can avoid making a choice. Ultimately, time runs out or options run out and he or she has no alternative but to choose a moral side or lose absolutely.

When selecting examples for act three, or when creating additional ones, consider the progression of your plot and leverage the events to put your Main Character in a moral vice-grip.

NOTE: Some stories do not force the Main Character to make an active moral choice. Rather, the Main Character emerges from his or her experiences in the story having been changed or not changed in a passive way.

For example, in the movie, "Jaws," Chief Brody does not have the courage to face his fear of the water. He won't even go swimming, and when there is trouble along the shore, he stops at the waterline. Thematically, he avoids his fears, rather than confronting them.

Through the events of the story where he grapples with his fear, he is forced by circumstances to tread ever deeper into threatening situations. Finally, he must kill the shark while hanging onto the rigging on a sinking boat.

At the end of the story, as he paddles back to shore he says, "You know, I used to be afraid of the water."

In this story, he has been changed by the experiences of the story yet never made a conscious choice to do so.

From the material you have already developed, select the illustrations of your Main Character's Dilemma to include in act three that will bring the issue to a head and force the Main Character to make a choice at a "moment of truth" or will indicate that the character has or has not been changed without having made a direct choice.

~ Step 132 ~

Author's Proof

Through three acts and a climax you have argued your theme. Once the smoke clears, you need to draw your conclusions. This is the time that you confirm to your readers that they did, in fact, get your point.

Previously, you did not want to illustrate both the Message Issue and the Counterpoint in the same scene or dramatic moment due to the risk of your thematic argument appearing ham-handed, or one-sided. But now, your readers have already drawn a conclusion by averaging all of material about both sides of the argument together, just before the climax.

Now that all has been said and done, you need to reaffirm that conclusion by providing a direct comparison between the results of having employed the Message Issue and the results of having employed the Counterpoint.

Some of your characters used the Message Issue as their moral approach throughout the story. Others employed the

Counterpoint. The Main Character either stuck with the Message Issue or changed to adopt the Counterpoint.

Which group fares better?

Keep in mind this is NOT the time to make or even continue your moral argument. Rather, this is the time to show the tangible results of following each side. If you have successfully made the argument, your readers will agree with your conclusions, which will strengthen your point in each individual reader when he or she closes your book and returns to his or her own life

In this step, then, draw on material you have previous developed to create one or more scenarios that will illustrate the relative value of your message to our counterpoint by direct comparison of how the camps that followed each ultimately fare.

~ Step 133 ~

Theme - Act One Beginning

Theme is intriguing because it is the most emotionally powerful part of your story, but also the least structured. Previously, you have determined which aspects of your Thematic Topic, Message Issue, Counterpoint, and Main Character dilemma you wish to explore in acts one, two, and three.

Now it is time to get a bit more specific and divide each act's exploration of theme into Beginning, Middle, and End.

Act one is where you establish your theme. It must be done clearly, but gently, so as not to appear to ham-handed.

Don't forget that the thematic message issue and the counterpoint should never appear together in the same scene or at the same dramatic moment. If they do, it make your theme appear preachy as it seems you are telling your readers what to think, rather than letting them make their own decisions.

In this step, list the illustrations of your theme you developed for the first act that you wish to present in the *beginning* of act one to establish the method of development you selected from the three approaches (small to large, large to small, mixed).

~ Step 134 ~

Theme - Act One Middle

In this step, select from your act one thematic illustrations the scenarios you wish to explore in the middle of the first act that will continue the method of thematic development you have chosen.

Keep in mind that you should never bring the message issue and counterpoint into the same scenario.

~ Step 135 ~

Theme - Act One Ending

In this step, select from your act one thematic illustrations the scenarios you wish to explore in the last third of the first act that will conclude the thematic introductions and set the stage for continued development in step 2.

After this step, you should have no unused thematic illustrations from the material you created for act one remaining. If you do, work them into the beginning, middle or end of the first act unless they are no longer appropriate to the flow of your novel.

Keep in mind that you should never bring the message issue and counterpoint into the same scenario.

~ Step 136 ~

Theme - Act Two Beginning

The second act should extend your theme. By this, we mean that your theme should gain added depth and breadth as you layer more illustrations on top of the impressions you have already made on your readers.

Theme exposition might be to start with thematic impact on a grand scale in act one, then extend it to explore more personal issues in act two. Or, the reverse might be more appropriate for your story. Another approach is to alternate among grand and personal illustrations of your theme and use act two simply to build the breadth and nuance of how theme impacts your story at all levels.

In this step, select from the scenarios you already earmarked for act two that will grow your theme's impact in the beginning of the second act.

~ Step 137 ~

Theme - Act Two Middle

In this step, select the scenarios from those you already chose for act two which will present those aspects of your theme that will advance your thematic progression in the middle of the second act.

~ Step 138 ~

Theme - Act Two Ending

In this step, select the remaining scenarios you previously chose for your theme for act two that will advance the progression of your thematic argument in the last part of the second act.

If any illustrations remain unused from those you originally selected for act two, see if you can work them into the beginning, middle or end without negatively impacting the flow of your novel.

~ Step 139 ~

Theme - Act Three Beginning

The third act of theme is where you project your thematic message into your readers. You make it personal to them, not just to your characters.

Your previous examples should include those that tug on the heartstrings of your readers by centering on characters they care about most.

You've already determined which illustrations you want to appear in the third act. Now is the time to be more specific and to divide those scenarios s among the beginning, middle, and end of act three.

In this step, select from the illustrations of your theme that you earmarked for act three those scenarios you wish to explore in the beginning of the third act to continue your thematic argument.

~ Step 140 ~

Theme - Act Three Middle

In this step, refer to the illustrations of your theme that you previous selected to appear in act three, and choose those that will best support your thematic flow in the middle of the third act.

~ Step 141 ~

Theme - Act Three Ending

This is your last opportunity to make your thematic point. You may wish to use the ending section of act three to re-enforce earlier choices, or you may wish to alter the balance between the relative worth of the message issue and the counterpoint.

Refer to the choices you've made for the beginning and middle of act three and look at the scenarios and illustrations that remain to be presented.

Reconsider your choices for the beginning and middle of act three, and if necessary, go back and adjust them so that you end on the thematic note that will cap off your message in the strongest possible manner.

Then, list those scenarios and illustrations you want to present in the last part of act three.

Storytelling

Part Four: Genre

~ Step 142 ~

Act One Genre Elements

Your novel's genre is its overall personality. As with the people that you meet, first impressions are very important. In act one, you introduce your story to your readers. The selection of genre elements you choose to initially employ will set the mood for all that follows. They can also be misleading, and you can use this to your advantage.

You may be working with a standard genre, or trying something new. But it often helps involve your readers by starting with the familiar. In this way, those experiencing your story are eased out of the real world and into the one you have constructed. So, in the first act, you many want to establish a few touch points the readers can hang their hats on.

As we get to know people a little better, our initial impression of the "type" of person they are begins to slowly alter, making them a little more of an individual and a little less of a stereotype. To this end, as the first act progresses, you may want to hint at a few attributes or elements of your story's personality that begin to drift from the norm.

By the end of the first act, you should have dropped enough elements to give your story a general personality type and also to indicate that a deeper personality waits to be revealed.

As a side note, this deeper personality may in fact be the true personality of your story, hidden behind inaccurate first impressions.

Referring to the material you have already developed in the Exposition Stage, select the genre elements that would be best doled out in the first act to create the first impression of your novel's personality.

~ Step 143 ~

Act Two Genre Elements

In the second act, your story's genre personality develops more specific traits or elements that shift it out of the realm of a broad personality type and into the realm of the individual. Your readers come to expect certain things from your story, both in the elements and in the style with which they are presented.

If the first impression of your novel as developed in act one is a true representation of the underpinnings of your story's personality, then act two adds details and richness to the overall feel over the novel. But if the first impression is a deception hiding a different story personality beneath it, then act two brings elements to the surface that reveal the basic nature of its true personality.

Referring to the material you have already developed in the Exposition Stage, select the genre elements that would be best doled out in the second act.

~ Step 144 ~

Act Three Genre Elements

It is the third act where you will either reveal the final details that make your story's personality unique as an individual, or will reveal the full extent of its true personality that was masked behind the first impressions of the first act.

Either way, by the end of the third act you want your reader/audience to feel as if your novel is an old friend or an old enemy - a person they understand as to who it is by nature, and what it is capable of.

Referring to the material you have already developed in the Exposition Stage and what you have already chosen to appear in acts one and two, select the genre elements that would be best doled out in the third act.

Also consider repositioning some elements from one act to another to smooth the flow of your genre's development.

~ Step 145 ~

Genre Conclusion

If you've ever seen the end of a science fiction movie where the world is saved, the words "The End" appear, and then a question mark appears, you have experienced a last-minute change in the personality of a story's genre.

In the conclusion, you can either re-affirm the personality you have so far revealed, alter it at the last moment, or hint that it may be altered. For example, in the original movie "Alien," there are several red herrings in the end of act three that alternately make it look as if Ripley or the Alien will ultimately triumph. In the conclusion of Alien, the Alien has been apparently vanquished, and Ripley puts herself in suspended animation for the long return home. But the music, which has been written to initially convey a sense that danger is over suddenly takes a subtle turn toward the minor chords and holds them, making us feel that perhaps a hidden danger still lurks. Finally, the music returns to a sustained major chord as the ship disappears in the distance, confirming that indeed, the danger has past.

Keep in mind that your readers will need to say goodbye to the story they have come to know. Just as they needed to be introduced to the story's personality in act one and drawn out of the real world into the fictional one, now they need to be disentangled from the story's personality and eased back into the real world.

Just as one wraps up a visit with a friend in a gradual withdrawal, so too you must let your readers down gently, always considering that the last moments your readers spend with your story will leave a final impression even more important than the first impression.

Select from those genre elements you already or earmarked in the Exposition Stage those that will confirm the personality of your story and help your readers say goodbye. If need be, develop additional elements to support this effort.

By the end of this step, you should have no remaining genre

elements to distribute. If any remain, see if you can work them into acts one, two, three or the conclusion to further enrich your novel.

~ Step 146 ~

Genre - Act One Beginning

You've already divided your genre elements into those you wish to present in acts 1, 2, and 3. Now you need to get a bit more specific and parcel them out to occur at the beginning, middle, and end.

Keep in mind that the beginning of act one will be your readers' first introduction to the overall personality of your story, and will contribute greatly as to whether they want to spend time with your novel or put it back on the shelf.

Consider how the genre will interact with the teaser and the introduction of your character and then, in this step, list the genre elements you wish to present at the beginning of act one.

~ Step 147 ~

Genre - Act One Middle

The middle of act one indicates to your readers whether your novel's personality is superficial or has some depth to it. Take this opportunity to add a few unexpected elements into the mix, even while supporting the initial personality type.

If,, however, you intentionally chose to mislead your readers as to your story's personality, the middle of act one is where you may wish to add elements that don't quite fit and hint that the true genre personality of your novel may not be what it originally appeared to be.

For this step, list the genre elements you wish to present in the middle of the first act.

~ Step 148 ~

Genre - Act One Ending

By the end of your first act, your readers should clearly understand whether your novel's personality is relatively stable or will likely surprise them as it unfolds.

For a stable genre, the end of act one should include elements that support first impressions of your novel's personality type but add to or at least hint at additional depth and shadings to come.

For a surprising genre, the end of act one should include elements that fly contrary to first impressions of your novel's personality and add to or at least hint at a greater true and more surprises to come.

In this step, list the genre elements you wish to present in the last part of the first act.

~ Step 149 ~

Genre - Act Two Beginning

For genre, the beginning of act two is the opportunity to either reveal your novel's personality in significantly greater depth or to add elements that completely alter your reader's first impressions of its personality type.

In this step, list the genre elements you wish to present in the beginning of the second act.

~ Step 150 ~

Genre - Act Two Middle

Genre in the middle of act two should enrich your readers' experience with your novel's personality, either by adding shadings and nuance or by unveiling surprising inconsistencies that portend a greater truth lurking in the background.

Your novel's personality, like those of individual people, determines the mood and timber of its relationship to your readers. Here, in the geographic center of your story – the midpoint in your entire timeline, the one thing you most want to avoid is boredom – a sense of complacency that leads to taking the genre for granted resulting in a progressive lack of interest.

In this step, list the genre elements you wish to present in the middle of the second act that will add enough new depth, shock, or surprise to your genre to re-engage your readers' interest.

~ Step 151 ~

Genre - Act Two Ending

By the end of the second act, your readers should feel secure in their assessment of your novel's genre. Whether it is much like it appeared to be at first impressions or turned out to be something quite different, your readers should now understand the nature and scope of the mood and atmosphere you are creating.

In this step, list the genre elements you wish to present in the last part of the second act. At this point you should have no remaining genre elements from those you originally selected for all of act two. If you do, see if you can work them into the sets you've chosen for the beginning, middle and end of act two, if you can do so without damaging the developing personality of your novel.

~ Step 152 ~

Genre - Act Three Beginning

The beginning of the third act is your last chance (save for the conclusion of the entire novel) to make an astounding new contribution to your novel's overall personality.

For a stable, consistent genre, add genre elements into the mix that create an unexpected degree of depth all at once. For genres designed to be more surprising, include elements that shake up all expectations of mood (without violating emotional integrity).

The beginning of an act is always a good place to infuse energy after all that was settled at the end of the previous act. And act three, with two already established patterns behind it, is the easiest place to inject new interest and energy.

In this step, list the genre elements from those you earmarked for act three those you wish to present in the beginning of the third act.

~ Step 153 ~

Genre - Act Three Middle

The middle of act three is the easiest place to drop the ball in giving impact and import to your novel's overall genre personality. You've already put so much forth to establish and evolve the mood and feel of your novel that it is tempting to just coast along toward the climax focusing instead on plot, characters and theme.

Failing to keep your novel's personality vibrant at this point, however, will rob these other aspects of your story of an emotional background that gives them meaning. Without the active participation of your genre in the middle of act three, it is likely to become more superficial and perfunctory, hitting the marks without hitting the heart.

You don't need to go to extremes to avoid this problem – just to bring enough new and intriguing genre elements into your story at this point to add interest and provide an atmosphere in which your plot, characters and theme can breathe.

In this step, list the genre elements you wish to present in the middle of the third act.

~ Step 154 ~

Genre - Act Three Ending

The end of act three is where your readers and your novel have grown so comfortable with each other that your story will reveal the fullness of its personality.

As with the people we meet in real life, it takes time to establish a level of trust that has grown from experience. Psychologists describe this as the moment of *disclosure* in which, in order to carry the relationship to a new level of connection, each party removes the mask of persona to reveal who they really are.

This process is not without risks, in people or in stories, for it may turn out that the truth about a person we have grown close to is not acceptable to our own interests or mores. It is this juncture at which a relationship either dissolves or moves to the next level.

How confident are you that the true nature of the story you wanted to tell is something your readers will accept, after coming this far? If you don't have a lot of surety, perhaps you never want to crack the façade. But if you want to make your readers embrace your novel more as a family member than a friend, you'll need to show them a side of your story at this point to carry them to that commitment.

Look back over all you have so far revealed about your story's genre personality through acts one, two and the first two parts of act three. Then, list the genre elements you wish to present in the last part of the third act, either to remain friends with your readers or to become part of their family.

Storytelling

Part Five: Chapters

~ Step 155 ~

Act One Beginning Chapters

So far in the Storytelling Stage you have developed a detailed independent progression for each of the four aspects of you novel (plot, characters, theme and genre).

While each aspect now has a good internal flow, the task in this section is to blend all four aspects together into chapters so they work in unison to create the progression of your novel as a whole.

To do this, gather together all the material you earmarked for your act one beginning sections into one list so you can easily see all that's going at the beginning of your novel in your plot, characters, theme and genre all at once.

In reading over this list, you'll probably discover that you can subdivide all that material into subject matter categories. For example, some of the material may focus on a diamond robbery as it unfolds. Another group of elements may center on an argument between undercover cop, Tim, and his boss about how the crime should be investigated.

While both of these things belong in the beginning of act one, they really belong in two different chapters. And so, you might create two chapters as follows:

Chapter 1: The Diamond Robbery

Chapter 2: The Cops Disagree on Approach

Once you've named all the chapters you need,, distribute the elements from all four aspects of your story that your selected for the beginning of act one into those chapters where they best fit. You can always create new chapter categories if the need arises during the process.

Specific to Act One Beginning, novels often start with a "teaser," which is a gripping chapter that grabs your readers and draws them into the fictional world. This teaser may employ any number of story points or even incidental storytelling to excite the reader. For example, there may be an intriguing introduction of the Main Character, a thrilling action sequence, or an argument over moral issues among central characters.

No matter which elements you include or invent, be sure to pay special attention to the first chapter or scene, or you run the risk of losing your readers before your novel even gets started if the first chapter is too informational or too chaotic.

As you continue to build chapters for other sections of your novel, consider the use of flashbacks and flash forwards. Many stories are constructed to reveal story points in a different order to your readers than the order in which they happened to the characters.

A well-known example of this is the movie, "Pulp Fiction," which presents the action completely out of order, leaving it to the audience to reassemble the pieces into "character order" by the end of the story.

In an overall sense, the chapters in all of act one need to:

1. Grip the readers

2. Describe what the story is about

3. Introduce the characters

4. Set the mood

5. Outline the moral issues

6. Lead the plot to a major complication

For this step, refer only to the material you already selected for act one beginning including your plot, character, theme and genre elements. Read it through to determine the chapters into which you would like to sub-divide this material. Then, distribute all the story elements into the chapters you created.

If you have any material left over and can't find a way to add it to any of the chapters, see if you can move those extra story points into act one middle or one of the other divisions of your story.

~ Step 156 ~

Act One Middle Chapters

Now that you have some experience in sub-dividing the material in a section of an act into separate chapters, apply the same process to the material you had selected for the middle of act one.

~ Step 157 ~

Act One Ending Chapters

Sub-divide the material from the ending of act one into chapters. If any material is left over, see if you can redistribute it to other sections of other acts.

~ Step 158 ~

Act Two Beginning Chapters

Act two is where details appear, characters and their relationships grow, the plot thickens, and the story's message begins to emerge.

May authors have trouble figuring out "what happens in act two?" But with all the material you have developed for your characters, plot, theme, and genre, you should have no trouble. The real effort will come in trying to determine which story points to put in which chapters.

On the one hand, you don't want the middle of your story to droop. On the other hand, you don't want it to outshine act three and the climax. This is one reason you developed a major plot twist for act two in your earlier work. This shift in direction will add to the interest of the second act, even while increasing tension for the third.

The plot twist might occur in the middle of act two and change the direction of the story so that the characters need all the rest of act two to regroup or recover. Or, the plot twist could occur at the end of act two, and set things in a whole new direction as act three begins.

Character relationships might reaffirm themselves or alter their natures through conflict and companionship. The theme might grow into new realms or change the mid-term balance of the emotional argument. And the genre will bring out more details about your story's personality or perhaps reveal a different nature behind the first impressions.

So look over the material you have already developed for the beginning of act two and then create the chapters that will embody that material. Remember to describe the story points in each scene or chapter in enough detail to draw on when you use them as your guide in writing a sequential synopsis in a later step.

~ Step 159 ~

Act Two Middle Chapters

Sub-divide the material from the middle of act two into chapters.

~ Step 160 ~

Act Two Ending Chapters

Sub-divide the material from the ending of act one into chapters. If any material is left over, see if you can redistribute it to other sections of other acts.

~ Step 161 ~

Act Three Beginning Chapters

Act three is the build to the climax. Having changed direction in act two, you characters now begin the final leg of their logistic and emotional journey. Obstacles and personal pressures increase. Each scene or chapter should tighten the thumbscrews one more turn.

There are many storytelling styles, but in all of them, the last few pieces should fall in place just before the climax, so that all of your story's dynamic forces converge on that one quintessential moment.

Looking over the material you have already created, group your story points into specific chapters in an order that will start out slow and end at a crucial moment of maximum conflict.

~ Step 162 ~

Act Three Middle Chapters

Sub-divide the material from the middle of act two into chapters.

~ Step 163 ~

Act Three Ending Chapters

Sub-divide the material from the ending of act one into chapters. If any material is left over, see if you can redistribute it to other sections of other acts.

~ Step 164 ~

Conclusion

This is your wrap-up, send-off, and author's proof. It is the chapter in which all the remaining loose ends are tied up, all residual dramatic tension resolved. It is here your readers say goodbye to the characters and disentangles itself from the fabric of your fiction.

Pull together the threads of your plot, characters, theme, and genre to resolve all things still open. Although you can create as many dramatic scenarios as you need to do the job, the conclusion should be handled as quickly and efficiently as possible. In short, once the show is over, Elvis should leave the building.

~ Step 165 ~

Final Synopsis

It's been a while since you last revised your synopsis. In the meantime, you have developed a tremendous quantity of new material and organized it in chapters. The task now is to create a final synopsis that includes all of these changes.

Using your chapters as a guide for the content and flow of you novel, rewrite your most recent synopsis as needed to incorporate the essence of what your story has evolved to become.

Remember, a synopsis is not supposed to include every story element. It is intended as a high-level description of your story's world, who's in it, what happens to them and what it all means.

A synopsis is more like an extended summary than a literary work or a detailed outline, so just capture the essentials.

In the next step, we'll pull out all the stops….

~ Step 166 ~

Sequential Treatment

Major congratulations are in order! You have developed every element you need in order to write a sequential treatment of your story.

Unlike a synopsis, a treatment is a complete explanation of your story in the exact order in which every plot event, character interaction, thematic point and genre element comes into play.

The only two differences between a treatment and your actual novel are that the wording of the treatment is informational rather than literary and it contains no dialog unless it is so essential to an understanding of the story that a direct quote is required.

So, for this step, refer to your recently revised synopsis from the last step for the overall mood, atmosphere and flow of your story and refer to the material in the chapters you've created for the details and sequence. Use these sources to fashion a point-by-point relating of your story using conversational language.

While your treatment can be any length necessary to completely relate all the details of your story in sequential order, as a rule of thumb, most treatments range between ten and fifty pages, depending upon the length and complexity of the novel and how thoroughly you describe each story point.

Once you have completed this task, its time to move on to the final step – the actual writing of your novel!

~ Step 167 ~

The Final Step!

This is it! Step by step you have developed every detail of your novel from plot and characters to theme and genre. You have created overarching concepts and penned a point-by-point guide to everything that will happen and the order in which it will occur. That's one heck of a lot of determination and perseverance.

There is only one step left – to actually write the novel itself, just as your readers will experience it.

Use your synopsis as flowing narrative, your chapters as pearls on a string, and your treatment as a blueprint. Each provides a different angle on your novel – a different kind of guide.

Now, using all three for reference, start with your first chapter and tell your story from tip to tail with all the style and passion it deserves!

Don't be afraid to move story points around from one chapter to another, even at this late stage of the game. Inspiration doesn't shut off just because you have an airtight plan for your novel.

As long as you don't break any threads of logic and put things out of order, you can rearrange story points to make your progression more balanced, more interesting, and perhaps less predictable.

And, don't be afraid to add new material or take a different turn if you get inspired while in the process of writing. Happens all the time. The Muse never sleeps; she just goes on vacation for a bit every now and then.

Just be sure that any additions or changes you make don't violate the seamless flow you worked so long to create or open new holes where there weren't any before.

Of course, you will likely go through many revisions on your way to a final draft. But the work you have done in this step-by-step method has created the entire framework as well as much of the fabric of the novel you set out to write.

Well, that's it. I hope you have found this step by step method useful and inspiring. Now, get on with it and create what you've gone through this whole process to achieve: your completed novel.

Thanks for allowing me to join you on this journey, and best wishes for all your writing endeavors!

Melanie Anne Phillips

*****

~ Resources ~

This method used in this book is based on our bestselling StoryWeaver Step By Step Story Development software. You can get a for just $29.95 or try a free demo at Storymind.com.

If you would like some help with techniques for beefing up the telling of your story, you may find useful another of my books, *50 Sure-Fire Storytelling Tricks!*. You can find it on Amazon.com or on our web site at Storymind.com

If you'd like to explore other aspects of story structure, storytelling or creative writing, check out our blogs at Storymind.com/blog and at Dramaticapedia.com.

And finally, you'll find hundreds of free videos on writing on our YouTube channel at youtube.com/user/Storymind

CPSIA information can be obtained at www.ICGtesting.com
Printed in the USA
LVOW05s2239240913

353926LV00029B/1389/P